A

BRIEF

HISTORY OF WINTHROP,

FROM 1764 TO OCTOBER 1855.

BY DAVID THURSTON.

"Call to remembrance the former days."—*Bible.*

PORTLAND:
BROWN THURSTON, STEAM PRINTER.
1855.

Extract from the Records of the Town of Winthrop:—

Voted, That Rev. DAVID THURSTON be invited to write and publish a history of the Town of Winthrop.

A true copy.

ATTEST: J. M. BENJAMIN, *Town Clerk.*

WINTHROP, Sept. 23, 1854.

DEAR SIR: At a town meeting holden this day, the vote above written was unanimously passed.

Very truly yours,

J. M. BENJAMIN.

PREFACE.

It is somewhat difficult to account for the fact, that no record of any meeting, or any transaction of the inhabitants, while they continued a plantation, can be found. Considerable research has been made, but it has proved wholly unsuccessful.

The writer exceedingly regrets, that this work had not been commenced twenty years ago. Doubtless many thrilling incidents of early times might have been saved, which are now irrecoverably lost. Had the writer anticipated that such a labor would devolved upon him, he might have accumulated a fund of information, from which a more accurate, copious and valuable history might have been compiled. But no regrets will avail to call back the departed individuals, who might furnish interesting matter for a book, or bring to light the needed facts. Some pains have been taken, by conversing with some of the oldest descendants of the first settlers, and written communications from others, to obtain what, not only might be curious, but interesting and profitable. But the hope, in relation to this matter, has, by no means, been fully realized.

It is scarcely to be expected that, in transcribing so many names and dates, no mistakes should occur. I have given orthography to some words and names different from the town records. Whether the change has always been more correct than the original the reader must decide. For instance, where I found "Life

Foster," I have written Eliphalet Foster. For "Lear Every," I have written Leah Avery; for "Sessors," Assessors; for "West Enda-rum," West India, &c.

Some may suppose the pains taken to collect such a catalogue of names was useless. However, the labor has been taken, and no small amount did it cost. But I have not disregarded the advice of Paul to Timothy; for I have not "given heed to fables," nor "endless genealogies," for mine end "in 1800," and sometimes in the middle of a family. Some may be disappointed in not finding the facts agree with their tradition; and others, perhaps, will be as much disappointed in not finding their ancestors' names at all. But as far as the records and reliable tradition have given them, they have been faithfully copied.

The compiler tenders his very grateful acknowledgements to all those who have generously aided him by giving dates, names, or facts to be introduced into the work. He would make particular mention, among these, of Mrs. Metcalf the aged, Dea. Carr, Mr. J. M. Benjamin, the Town Clerk, Mr. Joseph Pope, Hon. S. P. Benson, Mr. John E. Brainerd, Samuel Wood, Esq., J. B. Fillebrown, Esq., and Mr. James Stevens.

The work has been prosecuted under some disadvantages. Possibly had more time been exclusively devoted to its preparation, it might have been better. Regretting that it is not more worthy of the subject upon which it treats, it is respectfully submitted to all such as feel an interest in the history of Winthrop.

DAVID THURSTON.

Corrections, p. 15, last line, felling for falling—p. 27, near bottom, inferior for interior—p. 32, 4006 for 00,00—p. 40, under 1810, May for Marr.—p. after 1852, Marrow for Morrow.

CONTENTS.

CHAPTER I.

PAGE.

Location, - - - - - - - - - - 13
Boundaries, Early Settlers, - - - - - - - 14
Grants of Land, - - - - - - - - - 16
Soil and Productions, - - - - - - 18
Social Habits, - - - - - - - - - 20
Scenery, - - - - - - - - - - 21

CHAPTER II.

Other settlers, - - - - - - - - - - 23
Chandler's Grant, - - - - - - - - 24
Incorporation of the Town, - - - - - - 25
First Town Meeting, - - - - - - - 25
Burying Places, - - - - - - - - - 26
Town Meetings, - - - - - - - - 27
Gardiner's Dam, - - - - - - - - - 28
Taxes, - - - - - - - - - - 30
Provision for the Poor - - - - - - - 33

Bounties, - - - - - - - - - 33
Valuation of Property, - - - - - - - 33

CHAPTER III.

Roads, - - - - - - - - - 34
Representatives, - - - - - - - - 38
Town Officers, - - - - - - - - 38
Moderators, - - - - - - - - 38
Town Clerks, - - - - - - - - 43
Select Men, - - - - - - - - - 44
Town Treasures, - - - - - - - - 47
Constables, - - - - - - - - - 48

CHAPTER IV.

Division of the Town, - - - - - - 52
Division of the State, - - - - - - - 53
Against Monopoly, - - - - - - - 56
Hardships of the Early Settlers, - - - - - 61
Patriotism, - - - - - - - - 69
Honorable Confession, - - - - - - - 74
Politics, - - - - - - - - - 77

CHAPTER V.

Standard of Weights, - - - - - - - 83
Pounds, - - - - - - - - - 83
Warning out of Town, - - - - - 84
Manufactures and Mechanics, - - - - - - 85
Banks, - - - - - - - - - 89

CHAPTER VI.

Education, - - - - - - - - - - - 90
Graduates, - - - - - - - - 97
Doctors, - - - - - - - - - - 98
Physicians who have practised in Winthrop, - - 100
Lawyers, - - - - - - - - - - - 104
Lawyers who have practised in Winthrop, - - - 105
Preachers, - - - - - - - - - - 107

CHAPTER VII.

Ecclesiasticgal History, - - - - - - - 110
Congregationalists, - - - - - - - 110
Friends, - - - - - - - - - 124
Episcopal Methodists, - - - - - - 125
Calvinist Baptist Church, - - - - - - 126
Universalists, - - - - - - - - 129
Christian Band, - - - - - - - - 132
Freewill Baptists, - - - - - - - 132
Houses for Worship, - - - - - - - 132
Ministerial Fund, - - - - - - - 140

CHAPTER VIII.

Morals, - - - - . - - - - 143
Winthrop Society for the promotion of good Morals, - 144
Temperance, - - - - - - - - - 145
Efforts made by the Town to effect a reformation of Morals, 148
Temperance Tavern, - - - - - - - - 151
Washingtonian Society, - - - - - - 151

CHAPTER IX.

Watercure Establishment, - - - - - - - 168
Marriages and Deaths, - - - - - - - 169
Genealogical Register, - - - - - - - - 172
Sons of Temperance, - - - - - - - - 152
Watchman's Club, - - - - - - - - 152
Anti-Slavery, - - - - - - - - - 153
Society for Mutual Improvement, - - - - 155
Moral reform Society, - - - - - - - - 157
Agricultural Societies,- - - - - - - 158
Kennebec Agricultural Society, - - - - - 159
Literary Societies, - - - - - - - - 161
Anderson Institution, - - - - - - - - 162
Franklin Society, - - - - - - - - 165
Lyceums, - - - - - - - - - - 165

APPENDIX.

NOTE A.

Deed to Early Settlers, - - - - - - - 20

NOTE B.

Act to Incorporate the Town of Winthrop, - - - 215

NOTE C.

Warrant for Town Meetings, 1772, - - - - - 219

NOTE D.

Names of the original members of the Congregational Church and the Covenant, - - - - - - - 221

NOTE E.

Vote of land, &c., to Rev. David Jewett, - - - 225

NOTE F.

An act to Incorporate the Town of Readfield, - - 227

NOTE G.

An act to Incorporate the First Congregational Society of Winthrop, - - - - - - - - - 230

NOTE H.

Account of ordination of Rev. Messrs Belden, Thurston and Sawyer, - - - - - - - - - 233

NOTE I.

An act to Incorporate the Methodist Society, - - 236

NOTE K.

Names of the original members of the Baptist Church and ordination of Rev. Messrs. Ingraham, Merriam & Powers, 239

NOTE L.

Names of the members of the Universalist Church, - 241

NOTE M.

Constitution of Society for the Promotion of good Morals 243

NOTE N.

Constitution of Society for Mutual Improvement, - 246

HISTORY OF WINTHROP.

CHAPTER I.

Location — boundaries — early settlers — grants of land — soil — timber — productions — scenery.

POND TOWN, as Winthrop was first called, was included in what has long been known as the "Plymouth Grant," or the "Kennebec Purchase." This grant, or purchase, comprised fifteen miles east of the Kennebec River, and fifteen miles west of the river; beginning south at Merrymeeting Bay, where the Androscoggin enters the Kennebec River, and extending up the river to Skowhegan. The south line of Pond Town was five miles long — the west line about nine miles — the north line seven miles, "more or less," — the east line had two angles and its length is not stated.

A hunter, by the name of Scott, had visited the ponds and streams in Pond Town, for the purpose of obtaining fur, prior to the settlement of any family. Others had also been in the place for the same purpose. Mr. Scott had erected a hut for his shelter, near the Cobbossee Conte great pond, on the land, which the first settler afterwards occupied. Mr. Timothy Foster, looking out a place for the settlement of his family, met this Mr. Scott at Cobbossee, and bought his cabin &c., and paid him thirty dollars, but took no receipt for it. The creditors of Scott hearing he had sold to Mr. Foster, some two years after, sued Mr. Foster for the money he had paid to Scott, put him in jail about six months and subjected him to other expenses.

EARLY SETTLERS.

According to the best information I can obtain, Mr. Foster came himself in 1764, and brought his wife and ten children in 1765. He pitched his tent about eight rods from the great pond, on the lot now occupied by Mr. Jacob Robbins. Here the first framed building was put up, and is now the porch attached to the house where Hiram Foster lives.

The next family which came was Squier Bishop, his wife and six children, in the Spring of 1767. They were from Rehoboth, Mass. Families by the names of Foster, Fairbanks, Stanley and Pullen, came from Attleborough, Mass. Though several kinds of game were plenty, the early settlers did not come to be hunters. They had other designs and employments. The few inhabitants came into the wilderness to provide for their families, for whom they felt a lively interest. Had they been drones, they would never have thought of coming to Pond Town for a living, nor have encountered the toils and hardships incident to such a situation. They evinced a spirit of indomitable resolution and perseverance by their efforts to rear up families in such a desert. But coming from that part of Massachusetts, where they had been accustomed to no other than old cultivated farms, they were wholly unprepared for the process of clearing the land. They seemed not to know that corn or grain would grow on unplowed ground. They felled the trees, trimmed off the limbs and burnt them as much as they could and put in their plow. In this way they obtained very light crops, and had it not been for their milk, game and wild fruit, they would have starved. How many years they pursued this course, is not known. But it was not until three brothers, Nathaniel, William and Thomas Whittier, came from New Hampshire to that part of Pond Town, now Readfield, and felled twenty acres of trees and went back. The next Spring they came and burned their fallen trees. It made a tremendous fire which alarmed some who had never seen the like. They cleared off what the fire had not consumed, planted their corn and returned to New Hampshire. Some thought the course these men took, bordered upon insanity. But the corn sprang up and grew. The report that a field of twenty acres of corn was growing and looked promising upon land that had not been plowed, awakened no small degree of curiosity. Not a few went quite a distance to see it. In the autumn, notwithstanding what the raccoons and bears had eaten and destroyed, they harvested a good crop. From this experiment, the emigrants from Massachusetts learned an invaluable lesson. They were taught how to raise corn and grain on burnt land. I have heard one of the early settlers say, that every day's work in falling, burning, clearing and sowing, yielded him a bushel of wheat. In those days, that was good wages. One of the three from N. H., it is said, brought a bushel and a half of potatoes upon his shoulders from Hallowell to his farm.

GRANTS OF LAND.

The township was not sold to a few proprietors who might speculate and defraud individual purchasers. The Plymouth Company, or as they were then called, the "Colony of New Plymouth," granted lots to individual settlers upon specified conditions. In examining the records of the Plymouth Company, I find that on June 11, 1766, a lot of land was granted to Timothy Foster, "one mile long and one hundred poles wide, containing two hundred acres." This was lot No. 8, as delineated by a plan made by John McKecknie, who appears to have made the first survey of the town. The conditions of the grant were, "that the said Timothy Foster build an house not less than twenty feet square and seven feet stud, clear and bring to; fit for tillage, five acres of land within three years from the date hereof, and actually live upon the premises himself during said term, or in case of his death that his heirs, or some person under them shall dwell on said premises during said term, and that he or they, or some person under him or them shall dwell thereupon for seven years after the expiration of said three years; reserving to this propriety all mines and minerals whatsoever within the hereby granted premises, with liberty of digging and carrying off the same."

Squier Bishop had lot No. 17 granted to him, the same day, on the same conditions. Eben. Bly had lot No. 18 granted to him the same day, on the same conditions.

Lot No. 10 was granted to John Needham, June 4, 1767, on the same conditions. Samuel Scott had lot No. 13 reserved for him; but Sept. 14, 1768, it was transferred to Samuel Needham, on the same conditions. Oct. 12, 1768, Abraham Wyman had lot No. 12 granted to him on the same conditions. Nathan Hall had lot No. 11 granted to him same day, on the same conditions. Jan. 11, 1769, Robert Waugh had lot No. 98 granted to him on the same conditions. Timothy Foster, Jr., had lot No. 5 granted to him, April 12, 1769, on the same conditions. The same day Phillip Snow had lot No. 30; Nathaniel Stanley, lot No. 18; Amos Boynton, lot No. 29; Peter Hopkins, lot No. 9; Benjamin Fairbanks, lot No. 6; John Chandler, lots No. 51 and 52 — all granted same day, on the same conditions. Nathaniel Floyd had lot No. 42 granted to him the same day. Stephen Pullen had lot No. 56 granted to him Dec. 14, 1768, on the same terms. Aug. 22, 1770, Ichabod How had lot No. 70; Joseph Chandler had lot No. 78; John Blunt had lot No. 22 — all on the same terms. Aug. 27, 1770, Billy Foster had lot No. 7; Aug. 12, 1772, Jonathan Whiting had lot No. 101; Joseph Baker had lot No. 213; Samuel Stevens had lot No. 139; Stephen Jones had lot No. 14, on the same conditions. July 14, 1773, John Chandler had lot No. 99; Elisha Smith had lot No. 134; Squier Bishop had lot No. 55; Unight Brown had lot No. 64; Jonathan Whiting had lot No. 200; Richard Humphrey had lot No. 83, on the same conditions.

July 9, 1777, lot No. 247, according to John Jones' survey, was granted to the minister, who should be first settled in Winthrop. The conditions were, "that he should continue to preach the gospel in said town for the term of ten years from and after his settlement, unless the said minister shall be removed by death before the expiration of that term; provided, nevertheless, that in case a gospel minister shall not be settled in said Town on or before the year 1780; then this grant is to be void and to revert back to this Propriety." This is the lot upon which Mr. John Kezer now lives. (See Ecclesiastical history.)

Also, July 9, 1777, lot No. 57, Jones' survey, containing about 200 acres, was, by the Proprietors of the Plymouth Company, "Voted, granted and assigned to the Town of Winthrop for the use of the ministry in said Town forever." (See Vol. 5, Plymouth Colony's Records.)

The township was surveyed by William McKecknie. It was laid out in lots one mile long and one hundred poles, or rods, wide. (See Appendix, Note A.)

SOIL AND PRODUCTIONS.

The soil of Winthrop is various. Much of it is of a superior quality. The land was well wooded. The higher parts were covered with a heavy growth of maple, beech, birch, hemlock and spruce. There was some red oak. On the lower land there was some pine, fir, and hackmatack. In the swamps was some cedar. In the meadows were the native grasses, upon which they fed the few cattle they brought. The greater part of the land is arable. It is adapted to the growth of the different kinds of grasses, the different grains, and all the culinary vegetables to which the climate is suited. Pears and grapes are beginning to be considerably cultivated. Apples, many of the choicest kinds, abound. The settlers began early to provide themselves with orchards. The soil was very congenial to their growth. About every farm has a good share of orcharding.

The first cider made in the town was from the orchard of Mr. Ichabod How, on the place now occupied by Mr. Moses Hanson and Mr. John Stanley. They had neither cider mill nor press. But thirsting for a beverage to which they were formerly accustomed as almost one of the necessaries of life, but had been now for a long time without, with true Yankee ingenuity they pounded a quantity of apples in a sap trough, and extracted the juice in a cheese press. In this way they obtained a few gallons. All the neighbors (and that included a long distance) were invited to come and partake of it as a rare luxury. Since the temperance reformation has led men to quit drinking cider so generally, very little has been made to use as a beverage. The practice of engrafting choice fruit has changed nearly all the orchards. Farmers now find the avails of their orchards the most profitable productions of their land. Nearly all the farms are small rather than large, and generally well cultivated and watered. Ponds, or, as some of them might with more propriety be called, lakes, brooks, and springs, afford an abundant supply of good, pure water for man and beast. The Cobbossee Conte great pond, which is partly in Winthrop and in Manchester and in Hallowell and in Litchfield, is nine miles long. Two others, one north of the village, extends into Readfield and is about six miles long; another, south of the village, extends into Monmouth, and is about five miles long. Upon the stream which passes from the north to the south pond is a cotton manufactory, a tannery, a grist mill, two saw mills, a woolen manufactory, and a large establishment for constructing horse power machines, separators, winnowing machines, corn shellers, and various labor saving articles.

The number of ponds partly or wholly in Winthrop is seven. These waters afford a variety of fish, the most valuable of which now is the pickerel, of which, till within a few years, there were none. Some anglers caught several pickerel and put them into some of the ponds, and they have become quite numerous. It has been said no fish of this kind was found in any of the waters emptying into the Kennebec River from the west. The early settlers found the streams crowded with alewives every spring; but after the mill dam at Cobbossee Conte was made, the fish were prevented from coming up.

SOCIAL HABITS.

The first settlers in a new country cultivate the social affections. There are reasons for this. They leave the greater number of their relatives and acquaintance, so that they can seldom have personal intercourse with them. They often are at a considerable distance from each other; but they know all about each other's affairs, and have a lively interest in each other's welfare. When they meet at each other's houses, they feel entirely at home. As an illustration of this principle, the following anecdote has been related. Mr. Fairbanks one morning saddled and pillioned his horse (for they had no other way of riding) and rode up to Mr. Wood's and says, "Mrs. Wood, I came to ask you to go and pass the day at our house." Mrs. Wood says, "Mr. Fairbanks,

I cannot go to-day, for I am just kneading a batch of rye and Indian bread, which I must bake." "Oh! Mrs. Wood, that need be no reason. I can take you on the pillion, and the bread trough before me, and you can bake at our house just as well as here." So Mrs. Wood decided to go, and soon they were mounted on the horse, Mrs. Wood upon the pillion behind Mr. Fairbanks, and he took the bread trough containing the dough before him, and they went safely. Mr. Fairbanks heated up his oven, and Mrs. Wood baked her bread very nicely, had a very sociable, friendly visit, and returned at eve in the same way, with a good batch of bread. But what a spectacle it would now present to see a horse, saddled and pillioned, carrying a gentleman and lady on his back, the gentleman having before him a kneading trough,* in which was dough for a batch of bread! Yet had you lived in the latter part of the last century, you might have witnessed such a sight in Pond Town.

Such were their privations and want of conveniences, that a lady, in order to make her soap one year, had to carry her materials on foot a distance of three miles, to a neighbor's who had the necessary utensils.

SCENERY.

Some of the scenery is surpassingly beautiful. The

*A pillion was a large cushion for a woman to ride upon behind a man on horseback. It was covered with a cloth of sufficient size to keep the lady's clothes from the horse. It had on the nigh side a stirrup for the lady's feet, so that she rode side foremost.

Kneading troughs were of different sizes, from two to three feet in length, from ten to fifteen inches in width, and about the same height, into which they sifted their meal, and in which they kneaded their dough.

handsome sheets of water render it very pleasant. The ground rises considerably in passing north from the great Cobbossee Conte pond. From several residences you have an extensive view of that charming lake, dotted with islands of various shapes and sizes, which is exceedingly delightful. The scenery in the region of the narrow's pond is very fine. Lovers of interesting natural scenery, who have visited the place, have always spoken of it with much satisfaction. There are a few, and might be many, splendid country seats. The late Hon. Benjamin Vaughan of Hallowell, who, prior to coming to the United States, had held a seat in the British Parliament, when his friends from New York, Philadelphia, &c., visited him, was accustomed to give them a ride to Winthrop. They would come up the old road by the town house, and return by the narrow's pond. I have heard him say it was the most interesting scenery he had found in New England. From the hill on which the town house stands, when the air is favorable, the hills in Dixmont, seventeen miles west of the Penobscot River, can be seen, and a section of the White Mountains in New Hampshire.

CHAPTER II.

Other settlers—Mr. Chandler—the first road—first mill—Incorporation of the town—town meetings—Dr. Gardiner's Dam—taxes—paupers—bounties—acres of land and water—valuation.

In 1766, some young men, among whom were Stephen Pullen, Nathaniel Stanley, Benjamin Fairbanks, and probably Ebenezer Bly, came to the place; perhaps some others. In 1767, Nathaniel Fairbanks came and passed the summer, and returned. In the spring John Chandler came and a number of others. Prior to this, there was no road from Pond Town to the Kennebec River. The bushes were cut away, and a line of spotted trees was their guide through the dense forest. A grist mill had been erected on the Cobbossee Conte stream, in what is now Gardiner, by Dr. Gardiner and son, of Boston. The people had to go all the way to Cobbossee to procure the grinding of all their meal. Nor had they any other way of conveying it except upon their shoulders, for there was not a horse in the town, and there being no roads, they could not avail themselves of the labors of their oxen. An incident has been related as having occurred during this period of privation and trial, which may interest the ladies. In those days they were accustomed to all sorts of toil and hardship. Mrs. Foster, wife of the first settler, undertook to assist her hasbaud by going to Cobbossee to mill. Living on the margin of the great pond, she crossed in a canoe, to save distance, and the boat was taken back. By some means she was detained so long, that on her return to the east side of the pond it was so dark that she could not find the horn which was kept to call for the boat, and so was under the painful necessity of remaining all night in the woods. How many females in these days have either the strength or the courage for such an adventure?

Mr. John Chandler came with his family to the place in 1767. He had considerable property. Amos Stevens, then a young man eighteen years old, came with him as a hired man. Some two or three years later, his father, Joseph Stevens, removed into the place with the rest of the family. They were from New Ipswich, N. H. Mr. Chandler was also from the same place, and his was the fourth family which settled in Pond Town. As yet they had no road to the Kennebec River, and there being no saw mill in the place, they dwelt in log houses. In 1768 a road was cleared out so that they could pass with oxen and cart wheels to the Hook, now Hallowell. Mr. Chandler built a saw mill on the stream where the cotton manufactory now stands, and in the course of this year erected a grist mill. But to get the mill stones from the river was a great achievement. It is said to have required "the whole strength of the place, both in men and oxen, during nearly a week." For his encouragement to settle and build these mills, he had the grant of what is contained in the following document:

Copy of the conditional grant of land to Mr. John Chandler.

"We the Subscribers, the Committee of the Kennebec

Purchase from the late Colony of New Plymouth, Do hereby agree that Mr. John Chandler shall have a grant of two lots of land, of two hundred acres each, near the mill stream in Pond Town, and also one other lot in some other place in said Township, upon Condition that he gives bonds to build a Saw Mill in one year, and a Grist Mill in three years, and make one settlement on the said 400 acres, and another settlement on the 200 acre lott, both on the conditions aforesaid.

BOSTON, June 11, 1767.

James Bowdoin
James Pitts
Benj. Hallowell
Silv. Gardiner
John Hancock

INCORPORATION OF THE TOWN.

Pond Town was incorporated by the name of WINTHROP by the Legislature of Massachusetts, the 26th of April, 1771. On the same day Hallowell, Vassalborough and Winslow were incorporated. These were the first towns incorporated within what is now the County of Kennebec. James Howard, Esq., was authorized to issue a warrant to call the

FIRST TOWN MEETING

under the act of incorporation. (See Appendix, Note B.) The warrant is dated "the sixth day of May, 1771, at Fort Weston. James Howard, Justice of the peace." Under this warrant a meeting was "held the 20th of May, at 8 o'clock in the morning, at the house of Squier Bishop, Innholder. Ichabod How chosen Moderator to manage said meeting. John Chandler, Timothy Foster, Ichabod How, Robert Waugh and Jonathan Whiting chosen Selectmen. Jonathan Whiting chosen Town Clerk. Stephen Pullen was chosen Constable. Ichabod How, Gideon Lambert and Jonathan Whiting chosen Assessors. Jonathan Whiting chosen Treasurer. Gideon Lambert and Josiah Hall chosen Wardens. Abraham Wyman and Gideon Lambert, chosen Surveyors of highways." The leaf upon which "the Warrant" and the further proceedings of the first town meeting were recorded, is torn and parts of it lost.

BURYING PLACES.

At a town meeting, May 27, 1771, the Selectmen, according to instructions, "reported a burying place." The spot which they judged would best "commode the present inhabitants, lies upon the highway between Mr. Bishop's and Mr. Cha—[record torn off,]—on Mr. Pullen's lot, bounded southerly on said highway. The land contains one acre, lying in a square form. Timothy Foster, Ichabod How, Jonathan Whiting, Selectmen."

The next cemetery was laid out March 10, 1777. Micajah Dudley, John Chandler, Timothy Foster, James Craig, and Ransford Smith, were appointed a committee to select suitable places for burying the dead.

"March 18, 1780, Voted to accept one acre of land for a burying place, near Mr. Chandler's, part Mr. Chandler's, and part Mr. Lambert's, and part common land, as it is bounded by the committee." This is the cemetery at the village.

June, 1795, a committee of nine were appointed to select places for burying the dead, and to see on what terms suitable places could be had. The town records contain no report of this committee. In August, the same year, the town chose a committee of three to see on what conditions the town can have burying places. They were instructed to purchase three, one of Mr. Stephen Pullen, one of Mr. John Chandler, and one of Mr. Benjamin Fairbanks.

There are now five places for the interment of the dead, in the town, one in East Winthrop, one in the south-east part of the town, another in the Metcalf neighborhood, which was the first, one at the village, and another west of the village, near Dea. Stanley's.

TOWN MEETINGS.

The next meeting of the town was held at the house of 'Squier Bishop, Nov. 17, 1771, and among other transactions recorded, "the town ordered John Needham, Gideon Lambert, and Ephraim Lain, [Lane,] into the box, to serve as petit jurors at the Interior Court of Common Pleas."

They also voted to make and repair their highways by

a tax, and to grant £50 for that purpose the ensuing year. In working out this sum, a man was to be allowed four shillings per day, and oxen two shillings. "The Assessors, in levying the money for the highway," were instructed "to go by this rule, that a poll shall pay equal to £15 of valuation."

The next town meeting, as far as can be gathered from the town records, was held at the same place, Monday, March 2d, 1772. Mr. John Blunt, Moderator, Jonathan Whiting, Clerk. (See Appendix, Note C.)

GARDINER'S DAM.

Mr. Gardiner's dam, at Cobbossee Conte, was a great annoyance. It deprived the citizens of some of their means of subsistence, as well as a source of income. It prevented the fish from coming up into the brooks and ponds, as they previously did in great abundance. It is not known at what time the dam was built across the Cobbossee Conte stream, at what is now Gardiner. The waters of the various ponds and brooks in town find their way to the Kennebec river by the Cobbossee Conte stream, at Gardiner. The dam must have been built early, because the first settlers in Winthrop went there to have their grain ground. The first action of the people of Winthrop in relation to the dam, on record, is at a meeting of the town, Nov. 17, 1771, when they chose James Craig, Jonathan Whiting, and Ichabod How, a committee to solicit Dr. Gardiner & Son to open a place through, or around their mill dam, to let the fish up for the benefit of the town. In the warrant for the meeting, March, 1772, the 5th article was, "To choose a committee to solicit Mr. William Gardiner to open a place through or round his mill dam, to let the fish up for the benefit of the town." August 30, 1773, "The committee made a verbal report to this purport, that they had waited on the Dr., and desired him to open a suitable way through or round his mill dam, for the fish to go up for the benefit of the town, but that the Dr. wholly declined to comply with their request.

July 10, 1775, chose Joseph Baker, Ransford Smith, and John Blunt, a committee to obtain a fish way through Mr. Gardiner's mill dam at Cobbossee in some lawful way.

May 17, 1779, they appointed "Capt. John Blunt, Lieut. Jonathan Whiting and Mr. James Craig, a committee to the Court of General Sessions of the Peace to obtain a fish way round or over Mr. Gardiner's mill dam, at the next session to be held at Pownalborough in June next, and to pursue the affair, at the expense of the town, as they in their judgment shall think best, till they obtain said end, or shall be satisfied it is not attainable."

May 3, 1784, Capt. John Blunt, Robert Page, and Samuel Foster, were appointed a committee to procure a fish way through Mr. Gardiner's mill dam if possible. April, 1789, Benjamin Monk, Squier Bishop and David Foster, were a fish committee.

March 1, 1790, Samuel Wood, Joseph Metcalf and Capt. Nathaniel Fairbanks, were a fish committee.

April, 1791, Jedediah Prescot, Jr., Reuben Brainard and John Chandler, were appointed a fish committee.

April, 1794, John Wadsworth, William Pullen and Timothy Foster, were appointed a fish committee. May following, the town "Voted that the committee proceed against the mill dam, at Cobbossee stream, as the law directs." 1796, Samuel Wood, John Wadsworth and Elijah Wood, were the fish committee.

At a meeting, Jan., 1806, the Representative to the General Court, was instructed to oppose having Cobbossee Conte stream exempted from the fish law of the Commonwealth.

But all their efforts proved unavailing. No fish from the river came into the ponds.

TAXES.

The first tax, which was seven dollars, it has been said, was paid with the head of a wolf, killed by Mr. Benjamin Fairbanks. He received that sum as a bounty from the State, for the head of the wolf. Whatever the fact in this case might have been, there is probably a mistake in regard to the date. For Feb. 21, 1783, is the following, "Be it enacted by the Senate and House of Representatives in General Court assembled, and by the authority of the same, that whosoever shall, hereafter, within this Commonwealth, kill any grown wolf, or wolf's whelp, (other than such as shall be taken out of the belly of any bitch wolf,) and bring the head thereof unto the constable of said town, in which such wolf, or wolf's whelp shall be killed—the constable, in presence of one or more of the selectmen, shall cut off both the ears of the same, and cause them to be burned. And such selectman or men, and constable, shall give the party a receipt for the said head, expressing whether it be a grown wolf or a whelp; and upon producing such receipt, the party shall be paid and allowed by the treasurer of such town, out of the town treasury, the sum of four pounds, for every head of a grown wolf by him killed, and the sum of one pound for every wolf's whelp; and all such sum and sums of money so paid out of any town treasury, in manner aforesaid, shall be paid and allowed to such town by the Treasurer and Receiver General of this Commonwealth."*

March 1, 1773, in town meeting, "Proposed to the town that the Selectmen petition the Great and General Court to exempt this town from Province tax for five years. Passed in the affirmative."

During the Revolutionary war, the people were, in common with other inhabitants of the country, subjected to burdensome taxes. In 1778, the town "granted £30 to procure clothing for the army." They also voted "to give six dollars a pair for shoes, five dollars a pair for shirts, and four dollars a pair for stockings." They also "voted to raise 260 dollars, to be assessed and collected by the first day of Jan., 1779, to provide clothing for the soldiers. They also excused those who were in the army in 1775 from paying taxes. 1780, "Voted to raise three thousand pounds to hire men into the service, and that it shall be assessed as soon as may be." They agreed "to hire men into the service this year by a vote, when they are sent for by lawful authority." Aug., 1781, "Voted to procure 2850 lbs. of beef, agreeably to the resolve of the General Court—and 12 shirts at 12 shillings a pair, 12 pairs stockings, at 8 shillings a pair, and 12 pairs of shoes at 9 shillings a pair."

The town, many years, was very lightly taxed for the support of the poor. For there were very few who needed their assistance. 1793, Benjamin Monk acknowledged the receipt of $19 for keeping the widow Joy from the 5th

* Perpetual Laws of Mass., from 1780 to 1789, p. 367.

of May, 1790 to Aug. 12, 1793—and also for her clothing, £1 19s. 9½d. She died, 1797. 1798, Ephraim Stevens received $40 for keeping Joseph Stevens 32 weeks. Jan., 1800, Rial Stanly received $24,62 for keeping Andrew Nelson. Feb. 20, he received $22,38 for keeping Andrew Nelson and his wife, and for providing snuff and rum, and one shirt. This man belonged to Boston. For the bills for his support, amounting to $109,32, Dec. 13, 1800, were sent to Boston. He died in Dec., 1801.

PROVISION FOR THE POOR.

In 1837, an amount of revenue had accumulated in the Treasury of the United States, beyond what was needed to meet the current expenses. It was proposed to distribute this surplus in the different States. This town received as their share of the surplus revenue, the sum of $000,00, which they invested in a farm and buildings, bought of Jesse L. Fairbanks, for $2,100, for the support of the poor. This is a much more humane and Christian mode of ministering to the necessitous than was formerly practiced. They were put up at public auction and bidden off to the person who would keep them for the smallest sum. By falling into the hands of unprincipled, inhuman persons, the poor sometimes actually suffered for the necessaries of life. But now they are well provided for, and the town prospers.

BOUNTIES, &C.

May 7, 1798, the town offered a bounty of twenty-five cents apiece for every crow which any person should kill and carry to either of the selectmen. "Said bounty to continue one year from this day and no longer." 1799, the bounty for killing crows the same as last year. 1800, May 5, the bounty "for old crow's heads" was "fifty cents, and for young ones, twelve and a half cents, for two months from this day." May 6, 1805, they offered a bounty of twenty-five cents for the killing of old crows, and twelve and a half for young ones, from this day to the 20th of July.

In 1840, it was estimated that there were in the town, 16,880 acres of land, 8,342 acres of water, and 318 acres of roads, making the whole number of acres 25,540.

The valuation of property in the town in the year 1820, was $111,462,41. The number of polls was 376. In 1830, the valuation was $244,532. The polls 325. In 1840, the valuation was $459,380. The polls 340. In 1854, the valuation was $528,905. The polls 445.

CHAPTER III.

Roads — Representatives — Town Officers.

ROADS.

SEVERAL of the early settlers, from the spots on which they located themselves, appear to have deemed the elevated situations the most eligible. Apparently without any reference to the convenience of making their roads, or of harvesting the productions of their farms, they pitched their tents on the high ground. Their method was, to clear away the bushes to open a path from one habitation to another, and, with their ax, cut off a slice from the standing trees, at short distances, which was their guide through the woods. They called this *spotting* the trees. They not unfrequently traveled by this guide many miles, where there was no inhabitant. Without felling the trees to open a way wide enough for a road, they threw small logs across the miry places and the streams, so that they could walk over them. After they began to have oxen, they fell the trees and widened their path so that they could go with their cart wheels. They would, from one time to another, repair these paths, till at length they became permanent roads, of course they were very crooked and hilly. The town has been at great expense to render them more level and straight.

The first statement in regard to roads, on the records of the town, is dated Nov. 17, 1771, which was the autumn after the town was incorporated. "We the subscribers, being Selectmen of the town of Winthrop, this day laid out a road upon the height of land above Mr. Delano's, between the lot No. 4 and No. 5, and running across a range of lots into the highway, a little west of Nathan Hall's house, the road being about three poles wide, and the trees are all marked upon the right hand with the letter W.

TIMOTHY FOSTER,
JOHN CHANDLER,
ICHABOD HOW,
JONATHAN WHITING."

The records are defaced, and some of them gone, so that it is not practicable to give a correct view of the roads first established.

March 18, 1780, "Voted that sleds used by the inhabitants of Winthrop, in said town the next winter, shall be four feet and a half wide, from outside to outside, and all those who presume to use narrower ox sleds in said town the next winter, shall be liable to the penalty of *three dollars* for each offense. Squier Bishop, Nathaniel Fairbanks, James Craig, Francis Pullen and John Chandler, Jr., were a committee to see that this regulation was carried into effect."

"Voted to raise two thousand pounds, to make and repair roads, to be worked out at twenty dollars per day for men, and fifteen dollars per day for a pair of oxen."

March 12, 1781, the town "Voted to raise £4000 lawful money, to make and repair roads, and that men shall be allowed twelve pounds per day, and oxen eight."

REPRESENTATIVES.

The following persons have been appointed to represent the town in the General Court, or Legislature of Massachusetts, or the State of Maine. The town records are torn and some gone, for some of the first years after the town was incorporated. I have not been able to find any record of Plantation proceedings, nor choice of Representatives to the General Court, till 1775.

1775, Ichabod How was sent to represent the town in a Provincial Congress held at Cambridge, Feb. 5.

1779, Benjamin Brainard was Representative to the General Court. He was directed to procure a town stock of powder and fire-arms.

1780 and 1781, (Record illegible from bad ink.)

1782 and 1783 ,Jonathan Whiting.

1784 and 1785, Robert Page.

1786, Jonathan Whiting.

1787, Joshua Bean.

1788 and 1789, Capt. Solomon Stanley.

1790 and 1791, Jedediah Prescott, Jr.

1792, (Record illegible.)

1793, Samuel Wood.

1794, Nathaniel Fairbanks, Delegate to a Convention to be held in Portland in June.

1795, Jedediah Prescott.

1796, None.

1797, 1798, 1799, 1800 and 1801, Nathaniel Fairbanks.

1802, William Richards.

1803, 1804, 1805 and 1806, Nathaniel Fairbanks, Esq.

1807, 1808 and 1809, Samuel Wood, Esq.

1810 and 1811, Andrew Wood.

1812 and 1813, Samuel Wood and Dr. Issachar Snell.

1814 and 1815, Alexander Belcher

1816, Alexander Belcher and Samuel Wood.

1817, John May.

1818, None.

1819, Alexander Belcher.

1820, Andrew Wood.

The following represented the town in the State of Maine, after its separation from Massachusetts:

1821 and 1822, Andrew Wood.

1823, Thomas Fillebrown.

1824 and 1825, Nathan Howard.

1826, Hon. Thomas Fillebrown.

1827, Isaac Moore, Jr.

1828 and 1829, Hon. Thomas Fillebrown.

1830, Andrew Wood, and Hon. Thomas Fillebrown.

1831 and 1832, Samuel Clark.

1833 and 1834, Samuel P. Benson.

1835, 1836, 1837, 1838 and 1839, Dr. Ezekiel Holmes.

1840 and 1841, Nathan Foster.

1842, Samuel Wood, Jr.

1843, None.

1844, Francis Perley.

1845, None.

1846, Thomas C. Wood.

1847, None.

1848, James B. Fillebrown.

1849, None.

1850, Dr. Ezekiel Holmes. 1851, None.

1852, Ezekiel Bailey. 1853, None.

1854, Benjamin H. Cushman.

TOWN OFFICERS—MODERATORS.

The first town meeting after the act of incorporation, April, 1771, was held at the house of Squier Bishop, innholder, May 27, 1771. Jonathan Whiting was chosen Moderator. He was also Town Clerk, Town Treasurer, and Selectman.

1772. John Blunt.

1773. Ichabod How.

1774. Jonathan Whiting.

1775—Five meetings. Jonathan Whiting, Squier Bishop, Jonathan Whiting, Josiah Hall and Joseph Stevens.

1776—Four meetings. Ichabod How, of all.

1777—Seven meetings. Josiah Hall of the first, and Ichabod How of the other six.

1778—Three meetings. Ichabod How, Gideon Lambert and Ichabod How.

1779—Three meetings. John Blunt, Jonathan Whiting and Solomon Stanley.

1780—Three meetings. Jonathan Whiting, Eliphalet Foster and Solomon Stanley.

1781—Six meetings. Josiah French, John Sleeper, Daniel Marrow, Benjamin Brainerd, and Josiah Hall, twice.

1782—Four meetings. Daniel Marrow, James Craig, Jonathan Whiting and Gideon Lambert.

1783—Three meetings. Solomon Stanley, Jonathan Whiting, Jr., and Nathaniel Fairbanks.

1784—Three meetings. Solomon Stanley, Robert Page and Joshua Bean.

1785—Three meetings. Joshua Bean, Solomon Stanley and Joshua Bean.

1786—Six meetings. Solomon Stanley twice, Joshua Bean, Samuel wood, Solomon Stanley and Robert Page.

1787—Six meetings. Ichabod How, Joshua Bean twice, James Craig, Samuel Wood and Dr. J. Hubbard.

1788—Six meetings. Samuel Wood, Solomon Stanley, Robert Page, Squier Bishop, Phillip Allen and Dr. John Hubbard.

1789—Two meetings. Solomon Stanley both times.

1790—Six meetings. Solomon Stanley, Capt. Nathaniel Fairbanks, Solomon Stanley and Nathaniel Fairbanks three times.

1791—Four meetings. Joshua Bean, Solomon Stanley, Nathaniel Fairbanks and Solomon Stanley.

The following were Moderators after Readfield was incorporated.

1792—Three meetings. Samuel Wood, Phillip Allen and Samuel Wood.

1793—Three meetings. Samuel Wood and Joseph Metcalf twice.

1794—Three meetings. Samuel Wood, Ephraim Stevens and Samuel Wood.

1795. Samuel Wood.

1796—Three meetings. Joseph Metcalf, and Samuel Wood twice.

1797—Three meetings. Samuel Wood, twice, and Col. Nathaniel Fairbanks.

1798—Four meetings. Col. Nathaniel Fairbanks, three times, and Ephraim Stevens.

1799—Three meetings. Samuel Wood, Col. Nathaniel Fairbanks and Andrew Wood.

1800—Five meetings. Samuel Wood, four times, and Nathaniel Fairbanks.

1801—Three meetings. Andrew Wood.

1802—Four meetings. Samuel Wood, Nathaniel Fairbanks, twice, and Samuel Wood.

1803—Three meetings. Samuel Wood.

1804—Two meetings. Samuel Wood and J. Metcalf.

1805—Two meetings. Nathaniel Fairbanks.

1806—Six meetings. Wm. Richards, Samuel Wood, twice, Nathaniel Kimball, Nathaniel Fairbanks and Samuel Wood.

1807—Five meetings. Samuel Wood, three times, and Joseph Metcalf, twice.

1808—Five meetings. Samuel Wood, Nathaniel Kimball, Joseph Metcalf, Samuel Wood and Dudley Todd.

1809—Five meetings. Elijah Davenport, Dudley Todd, and Samuel Wood, three times.

1810—Three meetings. Nathaniel Fairbanks, John Man and Samuel Wood.

1811—Four meetings. Capt. Sylvanus Thomas, twice, Samuel Wood and Jonathan Whiting.

1812—Two meetings. Samuel Wood.

1813—Two meetings. Samuel Wood.

1814—Six meetings. Samuel Wood, twice, John May, Sylvanus Thomas, and Samuel Wood, twice.

1815. Sylvanus Thomas.

1816. Samuel Wood.

1817—Four meetings. John May, Samuel Wood, John May and Enoch Wood.

1818—Three meetings. Samuel Wood, Daniel Campbell, Esq., and Samuel Wood.

1819—Four meetings. Sylvanus Thomas, twice, Samuel Wood and Daniel Campbell, Esq.

1820—Four meetings. Samuel Wood, John May, Samuel Wood and John May.

1821—Four meetings. Samuel Wood, Sylvanus Thomas, John May and Samuel Wood.

1822—Four meetings. Sylvanus Thomas, John May, Samuel Wood and Joseph Metcalf.

1823—Three meetings. Samuel Wood, and Thomas Fillebrown, twice.

1824—Three meetings. Sylvanus Thomas, Levi Fairbanks and Thomas Fillebrown.

1825—Two meetings. Thomas Fillebrown.

1826—Two meetings. Thomas Fillebrown.

1827—Five meetings. David Eastman, Richard Belcher, three times, and Levi Fairbanks.

1828—Four meetings. Rich'd Belcher, Hushai Thomas, and John May, twice.

1829—Three meetings. George W. Stanley.

1830—Two meetings. Geo. W. Stanley and J. May.

1831—Four meetings. George W. Stanley.

1832—Eleven meetings. George W. Stanley, four times, John May, twice, G. W. Stanley, Samuel Benjamin, G. W. Stanley, and Samuel P. Benson, twice.

1833—Three meetings. G. W. Stanley, Elijah Wood and John Richards.

1834—Two meetings. G. W. Stanley and Gustavus A. Benson.

1835—Five meetings. Gustavus A. Benson, twice, Moses White, Esq., twice, and G. A. Benson.

1836—Seven meetings. Gustavus A. Benson, three times, Israel Bonney, Doct. Ezekiel Holmes, Israel Bonney and Moses White.

1837—Six meetings. Gustavus A. Benson, three times, John May, twice, and G. A. Benson.

1838—Three meetings. Gustavus A. Benson, twice, and Ezekiel Holmes.

1839—Four meetings. Gustavus A. Benson, twice, Elijah Wood, Esq., and Francis Fuller.

1840—Two meetings. Gustavus A. Benson and Elijah Wood,

1841—Two meetings. James B. Fillebrown and John Fairbanks.

1842—Two meetings. G. A. Benson and W. H. Parlin.

1843. James B. Fillebrown.

1844. James B. Fillebrown.

1845—Two meetings. James B. Fillebrown and William H. Parlin.

1846—Two meetings. Gustavus A. Benson and Alexander Belcher.

1847. William H. Parlin.

1848—Three meetings. William H. Parlin, twice, and John M. Benjamin.

1849. William H. Parlin.

1850. James B. Fillebrown.

1851—Two meetings. W. H. Parlin and A. Belcher.

1852—Two meetings. Wm. H. Parlin and Moses B. Sears.

1853. Gustavus A. Benson,

1854—Two meetings. William. H. Parlin,

TOWN CLERKS.

1771, 1772 and 1773, Jonathan Whiting.

1774 and 1775, Ichabod How.

1776, 1777 and 1778, Josiah Hall.

1779 and 1780, Ichabod How.

1781, Jonathan Whiting.

1782 and 1783, James Work.

1784, Nathaniel Fairbanks.

1785 and 1786, Jonathan Whiting.

1787 and 1788, Jedediah Prescot, Jr.

1789 and 1790, John Hubbard.

1791, John Comings.

1792, 1793, 1794, 1795, 1796 and 1797, Nathaniel Fairbanks.

1798, Samuel Wood. "Sept., he was chosen a Delegate to the Convention to be holden at Hallowell on the fourth Tuesday of Octo. next, according to an order of the General Court, to agree on certain lines by which to divide the County of Lincoln."

1799, Moses Wood.

1800, Joseph Metcalf.

1801 and 1802, Silas Lambert.

1803 and 1804, Joseph Tinkham.

1805, John May was Town Clerk until 1814, inclusive.

1815, Samuel Benjamin was Town Clerk until 1823, in.

1824, Seth May.

1825, 1826, 1827 and 1828, Cyrus Bishop.

1829, 1830, 1831 and 1832, Samuel Wood, Jr.

1833, 1834, 1835 and 1836, Pliny Harris.

1837, Samuel Benjamin.

1838, 1839, 1840, 1841 and 1842, Edward Mitchell.

1843, 1844 and 1845, Cyrus Bishop.

1846, 1847 and 1848, Samuel Wood, Jr.

1849, 1850, 1851, 1852, 1853, 1854 and 1855, John M. Benjamin.

SELECTMEN.

1771, Timothy Foster, Ichabod How and Jonathan Whiting.

1772, Jonathan Whiting, Ichabod How and J. Blunt.

1773, Jonathan Whiting, Gideon Lambert and Ichabod How.

1774, Jona. Whiting, Ichabod How and Jos. Baker.

1775, John Chandler, Timothy Foster and William Armstrong.

1776, Jos. Stevens, Jona. Whiting and John Chandler.

1777, Ichabod How, Tim. Foster and Stephen Pullen.

1778, Josiah Hall, Gid. Lambert and Eben. Davenport.

1779, Ichabod How, Wm. Whittier and James Craig.

1780, Ichabod How, Benj. Brainerd and Sol. Stanley.

1781, Josiah French, John Sleeper and Jona. Whiting.

1782, Jas. Work, Soloman Stanley, Nat. Whittier, Jr., Nathaniel Fairbanks and Benjamin Fairbanks.

1783, James Work, Nathaniel Fairbanks, Solomon Stanley, Benjamin Fairbanks and Benjamin Brainerd.

1784, Nathaniel Fairbanks, Joshua Bean, Solomon Stanley, Benjamin Fairbanks and James work.

1785, Jonathan Whiting, Benjamin Brainerd and William Whittier.

1786, Jonathan Whiting, Joshua Bean, Benj. Brainerd, Gideon Lambert and William Pullen.

1787, Jedediah Prescot, Jr., Robert Page, Phillip Allen, Doct. John Hubbard and Samuel Wood.

1788, Jedediah Prescot, Jr., Doct. John Hubbard and Phillip Allen.

1789, Doct. John Hubbard, Amos Stevens and Samuel Wood.

1790, Doct. John Hubbard, Amos Stevens and Joshua Bean.

The following were Selectmen after Readfield was incorporated.

1791, John Comings, Jonathan Whiting, Jr., and Solomon Stanley.

1792, Nat. Fairbanks, Sam. Wood and Phillip Allen.

1793, Nat. Fairbanks, Sam. Wood and Phillip Allen.

1794, Nathaniel Fairbanks, Samuel Wood and John Wadsworth.

1795, Nat. Fairbanks, John Comings and Enoch Wood.

1796, Sam. Wood, John Wadsworth and Elijah Wood.

1797, Sam. Wood, John Wadsworth and Chas. Harris.

1798, Sam. Wood, John Kezer and Andrew Wood.

1799, Andrew Wood, Moses Wood and John Kezer.

1800, Jos. Metcalf, Moses Wood and Andrew Wood.

1801, Andrew Wood, Silas Lambert and Wm. Richards.

1802, Silas Lambert, Wm. Richards and Elijah Fairbanks.

1803, Sam. Wood, John Kezer and John May.

1804, Sam. Wood, John Kezer and Nat. Kimball.

1805, Nat. Fairbanks, Nat. Kimball and Thos. Eastman.

1806, Nat. Fairbanks, Nat. Kimball and Isaac Smith.

1807, Sam. Wood, Dudley Todd and Hushai Thomas.

1808, Sam. Wood, Dudley Todd and Hushai Thomas.

1809, Sam. Wood, Dudley Todd and Hushai Thomas.

1810, Sam. Wood, Alex. Belcher and Hushai Thomas.

1811, Alex. Belcher, Jos. Metcalf and Elijah Fairbanks.

1812, Joseph Metcalf, John May and Peter Stanley.

1813, Joseph Metcalf, Peter Stanley and John May.

1814, Jos. Metcalf, Asa Fairbanks and Peter Stanley.

1815, Asa Fairbanks, Alex. Belcher and John May.

1816, Alex. Belcher, John May and Samuel Holt.

1817, Sylvanus Thomas, John May and Sam. Clark.

1818, Sylvanus Thomas, John May and Dan. Haywood.

1819, Alex. Belcher, John May and Silas Lambert.

1820, Samuel Wood, Benjamin Perkins and Daniel Campbell,

1821, John Morrill, Benj. Perkins and Andrew Wood.

1822, John Morrill, John May and Andrew Wood.

1823, And. Wood, John May and Wadsworth Foster.

1824, Hon. Thomas Fillebrown, John Morrill and Levi Fairbanks.

1825, John Morrill, Nath. Howard and David Eastman.

1826, David Eastman, Levi Fairbanks and Benjamin Dearborn.

1827, D Eastman, L Fairbanks and Benj. Dearborn.

1828, David Eastman, Benjamin Dearborn and Francis Perley.

1829, John Morrill, Samuel Clark and John Richards.

1830, John Morrill, Samuel Clark and John Richards.

1831, John Morrill, John Richards and John May.

1832, John May, John Richards and Thurston W. Stevens.

1833, John Richards, Oren Shaw and T. W. Stevens.

1834, John May, Benjamin Robbins and John Morrill.

1835, John Morrill, Benjamin Robbins and Sam. Clark.

1836, Isaac Bonney, Moses White and Oakes Howard.

1837, Alexander Belcher, Oakes Howard and Noah Currier.

1838, Moses B. Sears, Noah Currier and Francis Fuller.

1839, Moses B. Sears, Francis Fuller and Thomas C. Wood.

1840, M. B. Sears, John Fairbanks and T. C. Wood.

1841, John Fairbanks, T. C. Wood and Francis Fuller.

1842, John Fairbanks, T. C. Wood and Francis Fuller.

1843, Sam. Benjamin, Ezekiel Bailey and T. C. Wood.

1844, Samuel P. Benson, Francis Fuller and Jonathan L. Stanley.

1845, Samuel P. Benson, Francis Fuller and Jonathan L. Stanley.

1846, Samuel P. Benson, Francis Fuller and Jonathan L. Stanley.

1847, Samuel P. Benson, Francis Fuller and Jonathan L. Stanley.

1848, Samuel P. Benson, Francis Fuller and Erastus W. Kelley.

1849, Erastus W. Kelley, Oakes Howard and James B. Fillebrown.

1850, Oakes Howard, F. Fuller and John Fairbanks.

1851, Francis Fuller, Oakes Howard and M. B. Sears.

1852, Moses B. Sears, Zelotes A. Morrow and Stephen Gammon.

1853, M. B. Sears, Z. A. Marrow and Ste. Gammon.

1854, John May, Moses Bailey and Joshua Wing.

1855, John May, Moses Bailey and Joshua Wing.

TOWN TREASURERS.

1771 and 1772, Jonathan Whiting.

1773, John Chandler was Treasurer until 1784, in.

1785, Stephen Pullen.

1786 and 1787, Nathaniel Fairbanks.

1788, Samuel Wood.

1789 and 1790, Jonathan Whiting, Jr.

1791, Benjamin Fairbanks.

1792, John Comings.

1793, Joseph Metcalf was Treasurer until 1798, in.

1799, 1800 and 1801, Benjamin Fairbanks.

1802, 1803 and 1804, Nathaniel Fairbanks.

1805 and 1806, Barney Haskell.

1807, Dean Howard was Treasurer until1823, in.

1824, 1825, 1826 and 1827, Isaac Bonney.

1828 and 1829, Albert Haywood.

1830, Alex. Belcher was Treasurer until 1836, in.

1837, Samuel Clark was Treasurer until 1846, in.

1847, Gustavus A. Benson.

1848, 1849, 1850 and 1851, Alexander Belcher.

1852 and 1853, David Stanley.

1854 and 1855, Erastus W. Kelley.

CONSTABLES.

1771, Stephen Pullen.

1772, John Chandler, Timothy Foster, Ransford Smith, Joseph Brown, Robert Waugh and Benjamin Fairbanks.

1773, John Chandler.

1774, John Blunt.

1775, Billy Foster and Amos Stevens.

1776, Squier Bishop and Moses Ayer.

1777, Josiah Hall and James Craig.

1778, Zebedee Delano and James Work.

1779, Timothy Foster, Jr., "refused to serve, and paid five pounds fine," Gideon Lambert and Henry Wyman.

1780, Jonathan Whiting, Jr., and John Stain.

1781, John Fuller and William Whittier.
1782, John Chandler, Jr., and Benjamin Brainerd.
1783, Christopher Turner and Nathaniel Whittier.
1784 and 1785, Henry Wyman.
1786, Daniel Marrow.
1787, William Sleeper and John Comings.
1788, John Comings.
1789 and 1790, Henry Wyman.
1791, Samuel Prescot.
1792, Squier Bishop.
1793, 1794 and 1795, Benjamin Allen.
1796, Amos Stevens.
1797, Joseph Matthews.
1798 and 1799, Moses Joy.
1800, Enoch Wood.
1801 and 1802, John May.
1803, John Harvey.
1804 and 1805, John Comings.
1806, Benjamin Fairbanks.
1807, 1808 and 1809, Andrew Wood.
1810 and 1811, Ichabod Foster.
1812 and 1813, Samuel Johnson.
1814, Enoch Wood.
1815, William Richards.
1816, 1817 and 1818, Samuel R. Fowler.
1819, Cyrus Bishop.
1820, Noah Currier.
1821, Cyrus Bishop.
1822, Noah Currier.
1823, William C. Fuller.
1824, George W. Stanley.

1825 and 1826, William C. Fuller.

1827, Moses White.

1828, William C. Fuller.

1829, Isaac Bowles and George W. Stanley.

1830, Noah Currier and Isaac Bonney.

1831, Noah Currier and George W. Stanley.

1832, William C. Fuller and George W. Stanley.

1833, William C. Fuller and Isaac Bonney.

1834 and 1835, Asa Fairbanks.

1836, Asa Fairbanks, Elias Whiting and Cyrus Bishop.

1837, Asa Fairbanks, Elias Whiting and Cyrus Bishop.

1838, Asa Fairbanks and Thomas Newman.

1839, Jonathan L. Stanley and Cyrus Bishop.

1840, 1841 and 1842, Cyrus Bishop.

1843, Erastus W. Kelley.

1844 and 1845, Oakes Howard.

2846, 1847, 1848, 1849 and 1850, Moses H. Metcalf.

1851, Benjamin Thing.

1852, Benjamin C. Gardiner.

1853, Erastus W. Kelley.

1854, Josephus Stevens, Randall Nevins, Henry Woodward and Moses B. Sears.

1855, David T. Whiting.

The first man honored with the commission of Justice of the Peace, was Jonathan Whiting, Senior.

The next was Robert Page, in what is now Readfield. Nathaniel Fairbanks and Samuel Wood received the same commissions at an early period.

Samuel Wood was appointed Coroner, for the County of Lincoln, in 1789, by his Excellency John Hancock, then Governor of Mass. Lincoln County then included what is now a part of Waldo, of Sagadahoc, the whole of Kennebec, a part of Franklin and the whole of Somerset, if no more. He had the commission of Justice of the Peace prior to 1798. He was appointed Session Justice of the Circuit Court of Common Pleas, by his Excellency Caleb Strong, Governor of Mass., in 1814, and was constituted Chief Justice of the Court of Sessions by his Excellency John Brooks, Governor of Mass.

Nathaniel Fairbanks received a Captain's commission from his Excellency Governor Hancock, in 1788. He was the first, within what is now Winthrop, who was commissioned Colonel of a Regiment. Simon Page had previously been appointed Lieut. Colonel. Col. F. was probably commissioned as Justice of the Peace prior to 1796.

CHAPTER IV.

Division of the Town—division of the State—against monopoly —privations, hardships, &c.,—patriotism—politics.

DIVISION OF THE TOWN.

THE subject of dividing the town began to be discussed at least ten years before it was effected. Nov., 1781, they agreed to "divide the town into two parts, as the water divides it, i. e., the south pond, so called, the mill stream, the mill pond, and from the most northerly part of the mill pond, a north line to the end of the town."

In Sept., 1787, they voted again to divide the town, by an east and west line, according to a division of the town into two parishes, in Jan., 1785; and "to send by Mr. Bean, their representative to the General Court, to have it effected." Dec., 1788, they again voted to divide it "by an east and west line, as heretofore, 43 in favor, and none against it."

At the town meeting at the house of Henry Wyman, June 21, 1790, "Voted to divide the town into two towns, by an east and west line, leaving 5-9 of the space betwixt the north and south line, in the south town, and 4-9 in the north town. Adjourned to the green at the door. Voted to take the yeas and nays of the meeting, (on the question of dividing the town,) and also the yeas and nays of the town at large. Of the meeting, there were 37 yeas and one nay. Then adjourned to the house, and voted that the Selectmen prepare a petition to the General Court, praying for said division." This was done, and the north part was incorporated by the name of Readfield, in March, 1791.

The subject of having a town incorporated so that what has long been called the "Forks of the Road" should be the center, began to be agitated as early as 1809. It was contemplated to take a part of Winthrop, Readfield, Augusta and Hallowell, to constitute this new town. On the 8th of Dec., that year, the town voted to remonstrate against the petition of Jesse Robinson and others, for having the easterly part of the town set off, 58 to 18. At a meeting of the town, Dec. 6, 1811, they "voted that the Selectmen draft a remonstrance against the prayer of the petition of William Richards and others for a division of the town, and forward it to the Legislature the present winter session."

DIVISION OF THE STATE.

"On a Thanksgiving day, Decemr. 15, 1785, by virtue of a circular letter received from Hallowell, the inhabitants of the town of Winthrop were warned to meet at the house of Squier Bishop, on Monday, the 19th day of this inst., at one o'clock, to try the minds of the town respecting these three easterly counties forming themselves into a separate State." The meeting was held accordingly, and they voted in favor of having York, Cumberland and Lincoln Counties become a State separate from Massachusetts. They appointed Jonathan Whiting a Delegate to attend a Convention on the subject, to be holden at Falmouth on the first Wednesday of Jan., 1786, and to pay the delegate for his attendance. What was done at this Convention is not known.

"Feb. 8, 1786, Voted to have paper money made for currency and to pay rates."

March 13. This year Mr. Joshua Bean was chosen a Delegate to attend the Convention at Falmouth the first Wednesday in Sept. next. At this meeting of the town, they "took an exact account of those in favor and those against the Convention, and there were 80 in favor, and none against it." This Convention was, doubtless, called to deliberate on the subject of having the three Counties, which included the whole of Maine, made a separate State.

At a meeting of the town, May, 1794, Nathaniel Fairbanks was appointed a Delegate to attend a Convention to be holden at Portland next month.

April, 1795, on the question whether the town is in favor of having the Counties of York, Cumberland and Lincoln formed into a separate State, agreeably to the address of the Portland Convention, there were 75 votes in favor, and 2 against a separation. 1797, on the question of a division of the State, the votes were 86 in favor, and 1 against.

But in the lapse of years, the views and feelings of the people in Winthrop underwent a great change. For when the question was taken at a meeting of the town in April, 1807, the vote in favor of becoming a separate State, was 36, and against it 86.

May, 1816, the votes for the separation were 77, and against it 81. In Sept., the same year, the votes were, in favor, 76, against a separation, 100. Andrew Wood and Joseph Metcalf were chosen delegates to the Convention on the division of the State.

May, 1819, the town voted that the Selectmen be instructed to petition the Legislature in favor of a separation of the District of Maine from Massachusetts proper, at their next session. The votes in favor of separation 69, and 45 against it. The town sent the following petition to the Legislature:

"To the Honorable Senate and House of Representatives of the Commonwealth of Massachusetts in General Court assembled, on the fourth Wednesday of May, 1819. The undersigned, inhabitants of the town of Winthrop, respectfully represent that, they view the separation of Maine from Massachusetts proper, as one of those events, which in the course of things, will ere long take place. Massachusetts is an anomaly in the Union — a State whose territory is disjoined and disconnected, by the intervening territory of another State. In a State constituted of territory thus situated, the interests of the different sections will often become different, and in some cases, actually at variance with each other. Such we believe has often been the case with Massachusetts and Maine. But Maine is now so far advanced in wealth and population, that she is well able to support a government for herself. The present quiet state of the public mind on subjects of a party nature is peculiarly favorable to the formation and establishment of a constitution and government founded on those principles, which have been sanctioned by the wisdom and experience of our most enlightened statesmen. Add to this the peculiar situation of the District of Maine, bordering to the north and to the east upon two powerful foreign Provinces, and presenting to the south an extended seaboard, exposed, in time of war, to hostile invasion, while, in times of peace, a local government would most efficiently promote the public welfare of the inhabitants of Maine. In time of war, it would be desirable, even in a national point of view, that there should be a local government within the District, able and willing to command the resources of the country, to direct the energy of the inhabitants, and vigilantly to watch over the general safety. So far as we have been able to inform ourselves, the decided opinion among the people of Maine seems to be, that the time for the separation has now arrived; that a further continuance of our present political connection would only be productive of increasing jealousy and discontent; and instead of being mutually advantageous, would prove alike injurious and vexatious to both.

The undersigned, therefore, respectfully pray, that the Legislature would take the subject into their consideration, and give their assent to the separation, on such terms and conditions, as shall be honorable to Massachusetts, and just and equitable to Maine. And as in duty bound, will ever pray."

1819. Alexander Belcher and Daniel Campbell, were Delegates to the Convention for forming a Constitution for Maine.

AGAINST MONOPOLY.

The following extract from the records of the town will be viewed as a curiosity in legislation: "Agreeably to the powers given to us, the subscribers, Selectmen and

Committee of correspondence of the town of Winthrop, by an act, [probably of the General Court,] entitled an act to prevent monopoly and oppression, have thought fit to set the following prices on the following articles, which are to be the prices until the 1st day of March, 1778.

Farming labor, in the summer season, 3s. per day, and found as usual, and so in proportion at all other seasons of the year.

Tradesmen and mechanics in usual proportion with farming labor.

Good merchantable wheat, at 6s 8d per bushel.

Good merchantable rye at 5s per bushel, after rye harvest, and 5s 4d till rye harvest.

Good Indian at 4s per bushel.

Good sheep's wool at 2s per lb.

Good pork, well fatted and of a good quality, fresh at 5d per lb., and salted at 8d per lb.

Good, well fatted grass fed beef at 3d per lb., and good stall fed beef at 4d per lb.

Raw hides at 3d per lb.

Good calf skins at 6d per lb.

Good merchantable West India rum at 8d per gall.

Good merchantable New England rum at 5d per gall.

Good merchantable maple sugar at 8d per lb.

Good new milk cheese at 7d per lb., and other cheese in proportion.

Good butter at 8d per lb.

Good merchantable peas at 6s 8d per bushel.

Good merchantable table beans at 6s per bushel.

Good Spanish potatoes, in the fall of the year, at 1s per bushel, and 1s 6d per bushel in the spring.

Tanned hides 1s 3d per lb., and curried leather in usual proportion.

Homespun yard-wide linen cloth at 3s per yard.

Tow cloth, yard-wide, at 2s per yard.

Mutton, lamb and veal, at 4d per lb.

Oxen able to perform a good day's work, at 2s per day.

Horse hire at 3d per mile.

Good English hay at 1s 7d per cwt. (i. e., 31 shillings and 8 pence per ton.)

Meadow hay, in the meadow, 19½s per cwt.

Good merchantable white pine boards at 24s per thousand.

Good 3-4 inch merchantable white pine boards at 22s per thousand.

Good merchantable hemlock boards at 18s per thousand.

Good merchantable oats at 2s per bushel.

Good men's shoes, made of neat's leather of the best kind, at 7s 4d per pair.

Women's shoes, made in the best manner and of the best leather, at 5s 4d per pair.

Good merchantable flax, well dressed, at 1s per lb.

Good tried tallow at 8d per lb.

Good 3-4 yard wide tow cloth at 1s 8d per yard.

Good yard-wide flannel cloth at 3s per yard, and striped or checked at 3s 5d per yard.

Good merchantable tobacco at 8d per lb.

Woman's labor at 3s per week.

Making men's shoes at 3s per pair.

Making women's shoes at 2s 8d per pair.

Good English turnips at 1s per bushel.

French turnips at 1s 4d per bushel.

Carrots at 2s shillings per bushel.

Parsnips at 3s per bushel.

Good vinegar at 1s 6d per gall.

ICHABOD HOW, TIMOTHY FOSTER, STEPHEN PULLEN,	Selectmen of the town of Winthrop.
ABRAHAM WYMAN, JOHN CHANDLER, JOSEPH BROWN, JOSIAH HALL,	Committee of Correspondence of the town of Winthrop.

A true copy, Attest: JOSIAH HALL,

May 30, 1777. *Town Clerk.*"

At a meeting, June 19, 1777, Mr. Ichabod How was chosen to represent the town in the General Court the ensuing year. "He engaged to do all the private business for the town, and to bring 100 wt. of gun powder, exclusive of any pay, except his pay as Representative. He received the following instructions, viz.: 'To well and truly represent the town in every circumstance, and to prevent any more drafts in this town, on account of our being a frontier town; to enforce an act entitled to prevent monopoly and oppression, and to prevent its being repealed; to do all in his power to have the Representatives paid by the State; to provide a sufficient number of arms and ammunition for the inhabitants of this town; and farther, in a private way, to take all possible pains to provide a young gentleman to preach with us three months this summer, on probation; to secure the land that the Proprietors promised this town on its being settled; and to stay at Court no longer than is of real necessity, and to forward some suitable form of government in this State, which may conduce to the peace and happiness of the good people of this State.'"

The Constitution which the General Court, (i. e. the Legislature,) proposed, did not meet the approbation of the inhabitants of Winthrop. For at their meeting, April 20, 1778, they "voted, unanimously, not to accept of a form of government sent to this town by the General Court." At this meeting, they granted thirty pounds to procure clothing for the army; and to call in all the powder delivered out of the town stock, and authorized Mr. John Chandler, Town Treasurer, to demand and receive it. They manifested their patriotism by exempting those who were in the army in the year 1775 from paying taxes. They also "voted to make up to the widow Taylor one half her husband's wages, upon her paying four shillings a bushel for Indian corn and five shillings a bushel for rye, reckoning all the grain she has had out of this town, and the selectmen are directed to buy the grain for her with money from the town Treasury."

Sept. 9, 1779, they adopted the measures of the late State Convention regulating prices. They chose Mr. John Chandler, Mr. Joseph Baker and Mr. James Craig, a committee to petition the General Court to lower the State tax. They also instructed the Selectmen to provide grain and beef for the soldiers that are in the service with Capt. Foster.

1780, the Committee of Inspection and Safety were John Chandler, Squier Bishop, William Whittier, Moses Chandler and Nathaniel Stanley.

"Ap. 10, 1780, James Work, Nathaniel Stanley, James

Craig, William Pullen and John Sleeper, were a committee to make an average in town respecting service done in the war. Voted to hire men into the service this year by a rate, when they are sent for by lawful authority. Voted to raise three thousand pounds to hire men into the service; and that it shall be assessed and collected as soon as may be. Voted to empower the above committee to hire the men now sent for, as cheap as they can." May 23. "Voted to adopt the new form of government as it now stands."

HARDSHIPS OF THE EARLY SETTLERS.

The privations and hardships to which the early settlers were subjected, were such as those who have always been accustomed to convenient and comfortable habitations and well supplied tables, can scarcely form an adequate idea of. So great was their destitution of the necessaries of life, that some of them were, at times, reduced to the verge of starvation. Indeed, had it not been for the wild animals, the fish, the native fruits, and the milk of their cows, some of them would, doubtless, have perished for lack of food. when they needed meat, some of the more favored ones, would take their guns and kill a moose, a deer or a bear, with nearly as much ease, as our farmers now go to the pasture and select a sheep for the slaughter. But all could not do thus, nor could the most favored of them always do it. As a specimen, Nathaniel and Joseph Fairbanks, in the month of February, took their guns, snow-shoes and dogs, and started off in a western direction, on a hunting excursion. Having gone a long distance, the dogs went up a hill and gave notice, that they had found game. This hill, they supposed to be in what is now the town of Leeds. The dogs had found a noble moose, which the hunters soon killed and dressed. But the day was so far spent, they could not return. They therefore buried their meat in the snow and camped for the night. The next day they took the meat upon handsleds and brought it home. This was a valuable prize indeed. The four quarters of that moose weighed *eight hundred pounds!*

Mr. Gideon Lambert as wan early settler. He and his family had to subsist one season from planting time till rye harvest, on milk and herbs. During this time, he fell *four*, and some say *six*, acres of trees, and prepared them for the "burn" the ensuing spring. He had been a soldier in the old French and Indian war. He aided in the defeat of the British army under the command of Abercrombie, 1758. He also served in the war of the Revolution, after he came to Pond Town.

Some families were so destitute of provisions, that one at least, by the name of Delano, subsisted, for a time, on boiled beach leaves. Others were without bread from sowing time till harvest. Some of them had nothing for themselves but milk and maple sugar. One neighbor sustained the children of another neighbor on skimmed milk. A woman said, the day after the birth of a child she dined on smoked moose meat and turnip greens. Her husband had gone to procure them breadstuff, but was gone longer than was expected. She had finished the last of their provisions. What could she do? Her neighbors could not assist her, for they were in the same predicament. She was greatly at a loss what course to take to save herself and the child. She adopted this singular method. She ate salt; that made her thirsty, and she drank more, and thus procured nourishment for her child, till relief came. The neighbors would hunt in company, and share the game between them; because there were times in which they could obtain provisions so well in no other way. Mr. David Foster, in the month of June, was very destitute of food. He went to a brook and caught a sucker, which, while it was broiling, gave a cheering fragrance. He dug up some of the potatoes he had planted to eat with his fish; but he found the fish very soft and the potatoes very watery. But they sustained life. Mr. Squier Bishop came with his family to Pond Town in embarrassed circumstances, poor and in debt. But though for a season they were greatly straitened, and at times much disheartened, he at length accumulated property sufficient to enable him to pay his creditors the amount of their claims. Rev. Mr. Eaton once came to "preach the gospel to the poor," and impart the bread of life to these few in the wilderness, called on Mr. Bishop's family and found them very destitute. Mrs. B. went to the pigeon net and obtained a competent supply. At another time, Mr. Bishop's family were out of provisions, and none to be had nearer than Cobbossee. Mrs. B. spoke to her husband about going to procure something for their sustenance. He was much discouraged, and said he was so feeble, that he could not get to Cobbossee, and they might as well die where they were. But the good woman, not so desponding, resolved to see what she could do. "Necessity is the mother of invention." She bent up some pins, procured a pole and line and bait, and took her babe in her arms and went to the pond, which was at no great distance, and soon caught as many fish as she could conveniently carry with her child. On returning to the house, she heard a rustling in one of the trees, and looking up, saw a raccoon. Now what shall she do? If she called to her husband to come with his gun, it would, doubtless, frighten the animal, and he would escape; or if she went and told her husband, the game might be gone. Perhaps some good angel suggested to her the plan; which was this. She took off some of her clothes, and some of the child's, and made such an image as she could, and placed it at the foot of the tree upon which the animal was, and hastened to the house. She said to her husband, "the Lord has sent us a 'coon; take your gun and go and shoot him." He replied, "he will be gone to Boston before I can get to him." "No, he wont; you will find him there. The Lord has sent him." Mr. B. took his gun and shot the raccoon. They fed upon the meat till Mr. B. recovered strength and courage to procure a supply of food. Thus providentially their lives were saved.

There was a time when Jonathan Whiting had grain. Several other families had none. Lest the neighbors might suffer, his wife put the children upon an allowance. He, to teach them to be economical in the use of their bread, would sell only a limited quantity to any one, lest some others might be more needy. The soundness and strength of his moral principles were exhibited in another way. During this period, approximating a famine, he might have had almost any price for his grain. But he affixed a reasonable price, and no consideration could induce him to take any more.

An aged man, now deceased, wrote me, that he had heard one of the first settlers say, he had lived a week at a time on smoked Alewives and milk. At the same time, he was under the necessity of laboring hard.

When Mr. Joseph Fairbanks and wife had five children, they took a journey to Mansfield, Mass., on horseback. The mother became so anxious for her children, on their return, that, bad as the roads were, she traveled fifty-five miles! Much as the roads are improved, there are few ladies now in this part of the world, who would be either able or willing to perform such a day's ride. There was a time when this family were reduced to such an extremity by the oppressions of a certain man, I was about to say, but he appeared more like a brute than a man, that they had nothing to eat or wear. She searched the house to see if she could find any thing eatable, and discovered a quantity of bran. She attempted to knead it, but could not make it hold together, even after it was backed. They ate it, however, and it sustained life till he obtained something better.

The men had to roam quite a distance in search of their game. Mr. Ichabod How, one winter, went into the neighborhood of Livermore Falls, on a moose hunt. He started three, two males and a female. He followed them until they came near the hills, where Mr. Nathan Kimball now lives. There was a crust on the snow, which bore him, but was not sufficiently hard to bear the moose. They at length became so fatigued, that the oldest male turned upon him; but he was so near that he could not discharge his gun at him. So he stepped behind a tree, as the moose rose upon his hind feet to strike him down; but the tree was so small that the feet of the moose brushed his arms as they came down, but without hurting him. He found himself now in a perilous condition. The moose, however, went back to the others, and Mr. How shot him. By the time Mr. How had reloaded his gun, the younger male came at him, but the discharge of his musket, prostrated him. He then felt relieved, for he did not fear the other, and soon dispatched her. He cut them open, filled them with snow, and returned home. The next morning he called on his neighbor, Mr. Gideon Lambert, and informed him what he had achieved the day before, and offered to give him one of the moose, if he would go and help bring them in. To this Mr. Lambert readily agreed, and he and his sons Ebenezer and Paul, accompanied Mr. How and brought home the venison. Thus the families were provided with meat.

Mr. Unite Brown and his son Jeremiah, went to hunt for moose late one autumn. By what is called the "Great Bog" they found and killed one. But the day was so far spent, that they were not able to return. The father cut wood, kindled a fire and wrapped his son in the skin of the moose, and encamped for the night. The cold was such, that the father had often to renew the fire, to prevent their freezing. In the morning, the skin was so much frozen, that the father had no small difficulty in extricating his son from the covering. The children of the early settlers, not unfrequently, went barefooted most of the winter, if not the whole. They might often be seen walking on the frost and snow with naked feet.

In the winter of 1785, as Capt. Timothy Foster, the first settler, was cutting a tree, it fell on his head, and fractured his skull so that he became speechless. His son, Stewart, went to Falmouth, now Portland, on snow shoes, for a physician. But he could not leave, and sent a trepan, doubtless with some instructions how to use it. On the return of the son, the indented part of the skull was raised, and Capt. Foster roused up and spoke rationally. But so long a time had elapsed, the inflammation had proceeded so far that he died. His remains were interred near where Dea. Metcalf lived.

A man by the name of Fish, came from Port Royal, now Livermore, to Mr. Nathaniel Fairbanks' to obtain some leather. It was growing so late in the day, and there being no road, and only spotted trees for a guide, he was urged to spend the night; but he could not be prevailed upon to stay. He took two bundles of leather and left, and perished on his way.

A Mr. Dutton, a hunter, had a line of traps on the streams and ponds up toward the Androscoggin River. He had been out examining them, and night overtook him ere he was aware, and he lost his way. He began to call for help, hoping he might be within hearing of some habitation. Mrs. Bishop thought she heard a voice. Her husband doubted it. She insisted that she heard a human voice. At length he went out and listened, and became convinced there was some one needing assistance. Mr. Bishop called, and the man answered. He then went and brought him into his house. All habitations, though but log cabins, and all tables, were open and free. All were neighbors and brothers. The spirit of caste found no place among the early settlers.

The wife of Samuel Wood, Esq., was fond of referring to their early poverty. The first pig they ever owned, she paid for by spinning linen.

The early settlers did not cultivate their farms as much as would have been for their interest. Too many of them went largely into the business of lumbering, and depended upon that to procure their bread and other provisions from Boston, or some other place in the vicinity. After the war commenced in 1775, and the British cruisers were hovering on the coast, their supplies were cut off. In the spring of 1776, they were in a very destitute condition. Their scanty stock of provisions was nearly exhausted. How to obtain a supply, became a momentous question. The inhabitants of the town were requested to meet for consultation on the subject. They decided to charter a small vessel and send to Boston, for provisions. This was an enterprize of no small danger. But they hoped, that, by keeping near the shore, they might avoid the large British vessels. Through the good hand of God upon them, their little craft performed the voyage, and safely returned with a cargo of provisions. These were distributed among the people. From them, through the blessing of God, they derived strength and courage to put an abundance of seed into the ground. The next year, they had bread and meat in plenty. They thus learned an important lesson. Henceforth they cultivated their farms; God smiled upon them, and they had a full supply.

Such was the scarcity of money in 1784 or 1785, a man who had occasion to borrow *five* dollars, could not obtain it. Some of his neighbors had accumulated considerable property, had a good stock of cattle, but had no money. Such was the depreciation of the currency about this time, that Col. Simon Page sold a pair of oxen for *ninety-eight hundred dollars!* The real value, in present currency, was about seventy dollars.

The people were, at times, somewhat terrified by the Indians, as they passed, in their hunting excursions, from the Kennebec to the Androscoggin rivers. But it does not appear that they did them any other injury. A party once came to Mr. John Fuller's, when he was absent, and Mrs. Fuller and two children had no others with them. The Indians had "fire-water" with them, and began to drink. This produced considerable alarm. But they delivered up all their knives to her, and charged her to keep them, till they became sober. They did this to allay her fears, telling her, they were afraid they should hurt one another. They were certainly much more considerate than many who claim to be greatly their superiors.

Other instances of suffering there doubtless were, could all the facts be known. Some of them might be even more grievous than any here related. These are given as a specimen. Well may they awaken, in the present inhabitants, the gratitude they owe the Allwise Disposer of events, for having provided so much "better things for them."

PATRIOTISM.

The inhabitants of Winthrop gave early indications of a becoming jealousy for their rights. They would not tamely suffer the mother country to trample upon them.

At a meeting of the town, Jan. 12, 1773, appointed in part, "to hear a pamphlet sent from the town of Boston, in which the rights and charter privileges are maintained, and instances wherein they think they are infringed [by the mother country;] with a letter corresponding with other towns." "Said pamphlet being several times read, considered, and deliberately weighed, it was proposed to the town, 1st. Whether the rights of the Colonists were rightly stated in the pamphlet? Passed in the affirmative.

2dly. Whether the several acts of Parliament and measures of the Administration pointed out, are subversive of those rights? Passed in the affirmative.

3dly. Whether it be not a matter of the greatest importance to us, that we stand firm and united, as stated in said pamphlet? Passed in the affirmative.

4thly. It was proposed that the matter of these our grievances be transmitted and referred to the consideration of the Representatives of our General Assembly, for the redress of our grievances, and the recovering of our charter privileges? Passed in the affirmative.

Voted, that a copy of the foregoing proceedings be attested by the Clerk, and directed to William Cooper, Town Clerk of Boston."*

In the warrant for a town meeting to be held Aug. 30, 1773, "the 1st article was to hear and proceed upon as the town shall think proper, a pamphlet, the substance of which contains the copy of letters sent to Great Britain by his Excellency Thomas Hutchinson, the Honorable Andrew Oliver, and several other persons, together with the Resolves of the House of Representatives, and several other papers; all sent to this town from the Committee

*Town Records. The pamphlet is not to be found.

of Correspondence of the town of Boston." At this meeting these papers "were read in part," but no record appears of any action being taken at that time.

Unwilling that any encroachments should be made upon their imprescriptible rights, and determined to have their liberties secured; at a town meeting, Jan. 25, 1775, Ichabod How was chosen to represent the town in a Provincial Congress, to be holden at Cambridge, the *first day* of Feb., 1775. They then proceeded to choose "military officers to discipline the inhabitants, agreeably to the directions of the Provincial Congress."

Ichabod How, Captain,
Jonathan Whiting, Lieutenant,
Timothy Foster, Ensign,
Josiah Hall, Clerk,
Elias Taylor, 1st Sergeant,
Gideon Lambert, 2d Sergeant,
John Blunt, 3d Sergeant,
Zebedee Delano, 4th Sergeant,
Eliphalet Foster, 1st Corporal,
Amos Stevens, 2d Corporal,
Samuel Stevens, 3d Corporal,
Daniel Dudley, 4th Corporal."

Ready to defend their inalienable rights in the true spirit of warriors, they "Voted to raise £13 6s. 8d., lawful money, to be immediately assessed and paid into the Treasury by the last day of March, next, to purchase a town stock of powder, lead and other necessaries." The town paid Mr. How £5 6s. 8d. lawful money, for his expenses in going to the Provincial Congress, and bringing the town's stock of ammunition. The times were now becoming very alarming, exciting and trying.

The war of the Revolution commenced. April 19th of this year, the battle at Lexington was fought. The report of this aroused the spirit of the young men of Winthrop. Not long after, Nathaniel Fairbanks, (known for many years after as Col. Fairbanks,) and eighteen other young men repaired to the head-quarters of the Provincial army, at Cambridge, " to defend their beloved country." Of these eighteen, four were sons of the first settler, Capt. Timothy Foster; Billy, Eliphalet, Thomas and John, who went a privateering, and did not return to reside in Winthrop. Elijah Fairbanks was another. The names of the others are not known. Nathaniel Fairbanks was afterwards in the Regiment under the command of Arnold, of infamous memory, on an expedition to Canada. But becoming short of provisions, that part of the Regiment to which young Fairbanks belonged, were ordered to return.

The country being involved in an unrighteous war, the new settlements were much exposed. Their utmost efforts were put forth to provide for the security of themselves and the public. They viewed their own welfare to be identified with that of their country. At their meeting, March 17, 1775, they chose Jonathan Whiting, Joseph Stevens and Ichabod How a " Committee of Correspondence to meet the committees of other towns in the neighborhood, to consult for the good and safety of this eastern country." This was done in compliance with a letter received from Falmouth. The 29th of April, they held another meeting, and "chose John Chandler, William Armstrong and Ichabod How a Committee of Safety to meet the committees of other towns in the county ,to consult the public good respecting coming into some way of procuring provisions and ammunition, and other necessary stores; and that said Committee engage, in behalf of the town, any sum of money they may think proper for such purpose." The constables were directed "to pay into the hands of the Committee of Safety the money by them gathered for the Province tax."

"Mar., 1776, chose Ichabod How, Joseph Stevens and Jonathan Whiting a Committee of Correspondence, Inspection and Safety. For officers in the Militia, Billy Foster, Captain, William Whittier, first Lieut., Josiah Hall, second Lieut., and Benjamin Fairbanks, Ensign." Who the other officers were, the record does not say. Then follows a copy of the Declaration of Independence, adopted by Congress, July 4, 1776. It was entered upon the records of the town by order of Congress, and a printed copy sent to the ministers of each parish of every denomination, "who were severally required to read the same to their respective congregations, as soon as divine service was ended in the afternoon, on the first Lord's day after they shall have received it." Ministers were not then as much afraid of having any connection with politics as some have been since.

The men of Winthrop seemed hearty in the cause of the Revolution. They were ready to adopt the closing sentiments of the Declaration, and "with a firm reliance on the protection of Divine Providence, we mutually pledge each other our lives, our fortunes and our sacred honor."

Jan. 15, 1777, Joseph Baker, Rainsford Smith and Amos Stevens were added to the Committee of Correspondence, Inspection and Safety. March 10, 1777, Lieut.

Abraham Wyman, Lieut. John Chandler, Mr. William Whittier, Mr. Joseph Brown and Josiah Hall were chosen a Committee of Safety, Correspondence and Inspection. April 21, 1777, Mr. Ichabod How was chosen Delegate to a County Convention to be holden at Wiscasset. "He was instructed to do all he can to hinder the Convention from sending any remonstrances to the Great and General Court, against their taxing this State; and if the Convention get a vote to send any, to join with the disaffected part of the Convention and remonstrate to the Court against the proceedings of the Convention; and if there is any other business of consequence, to act his judgment as he shall think proper for the good of the County and public."

HONORABLE CONFESSION.

" *Winthrop, Jan.* 29, 1777.

Whereas the subscribers, by declaring ourselves Friends to the King of Britain and talking against the cause of the United States, have given cause of uneasiness to our neighbors and townsmen, for which we are heartily sorry, for being now sensible that we were much out of the way and humbly ask the forgiveness of our townsmen and neighbors, and hereby renounce the said King of Britain and all his laws as unjust, and promise to be good subjects of the States of America for the future.

JAMES CRAIG,
ROBERT WAUGH.

Witness, ICHABOD HOW.

A true copy, Attest: JOSIAH HALL, *T. Clerk.*"

In the warrant for a town Meeting to be held May 30, 1777, the 2d article was " to consider the list the Selectmen may lay before the town, of the names of persons whom they know or believe to be inimically disposed towards this State, or any other of the States of America, and to act thereon as the town shall see fit; and to choose a man to procure and lay the evidence that may be had before the Court, in order to support the charges against them." The town records contain no account of any action on this subject. But, May 6, 1783, their ardent patriotism was expressed by voting, "that the refugees and declared traitors to the United States of America, ought to be for ever excluded from returning among us."

June 19, 1780, "Mr. Jonathan Whiting was chosen a Delegate to represent the town at a County Convention to be held at Wiscasset, in order to apportion the abatement of the State tax on the several towns in said County of Lincoln." Here the town Clerk's ink became so pale that the record is illegible. The next proceeding was, "Voted to procure 74 lbs. powder, 250 lbs. of lead and 250 flints, and that Mr. Chandler, (who was town Treasurer,) borrow money and give the town's security for one to buy the above articles; and the Selectmen were authorized to procure them."

Feb. 2, 1781, the town "voted to join Vassalborough and other neighboring towns in petitioning the General Court for some abatement of taxes laid on us; and that Jonathan Whiting, Benjamin Brainerd and Josiah French be a committee to meet the committees of the neighboring towns and to agree with them on the proper measures to effect the desired purpose."

The records contain a warrant for a town meeting, May 7, 1781, but no account of what was done. August

17, 1781, they "voted to procure 2856 lbs. of beef, agreeably to a resolve of the General Court, and that John Sleeper be employed to procure it." They also "voted to procure 12 shirts, 12 pairs of stockings and 12 pairs of shoes; the price of the shirts 12 shillings, the stockings 8 shillings and shoes 9 shillings." They appropriated £100 silver money to procure the beef and clothing. They agreed to have this sum assessed forthwith, and to have it paid into the Treasury "by the middle of Octo. next." For services done the town, they allowed William Pullen 630 paper dollars, James Work 1365 paper dollars, John Sleeper £1 2s. 8d. lawful money, Samuel Comings one bushel of rye, and to Jonathan Whiting £2 8s. lawful money."

Sept., 1837, they "Voted, that it is the sense of this town that Texas ought not to be annexed to this Union; and that the Selectmen forward a copy of this vote to our Representatives in Congress." Upon a resolve of the Legislature proposing to amend the Constitution relating to bail, there were 23 yeas and 83 nays.

At a meeting of the town, Sept., 1808, "Dudley Todd, Esq., Dea. Joseph Metcalf, Nathaniel Fairbanks, Esq., Samuel Wood, Esq., and Major Elijah Wood, were apppointed to draft a petition to the President of the United States to suspend the operation of the Embargo laws, in part or in whole, as shall be most conducive to the well being of said States in their present distressed and embarrassed condition." The committee retired, prepared a petition, which the town accepted, and instructed the Selectmen to transmit it to the President immediately. They also instructed "their Representative to the General Court to use his utmost endeavors to have such Electors of President and Vice President chosen as shall embrace those ideas that the good people of this Commonwealth entertained under the Administration of Washington."

POLITICS.

Something of the politics of the town may be understood from the votes given for the public officers. I find no record of votes for State or County officers till April, 1783, when his Excellency John Hancock received 15 votes and his Excellency James Bowdoin 1 vote for Governor. His Honor Artemas Ward had 15 votes for Lieut. Governor. William Howard had 23 votes for Senator.

1784, James Bowdoin, Esq., had 12 votes and John Hancock, Esq., 7 votes for Governor. Thomas Cushing had 15 votes and Artemas Ward 1 vote for Lieutenant Governor.

1785, Hon. Thomas Cushing had 11 votes and Hon. James Bowdoin 12 votes for Governor. Hon. Tristam Dalton had 15 votes and Hon. Thomas Cushing 9 votes for Lieut. Governor. Hon. William Lithgow had 23 votes for Senator.

1786, Hon. Thomas Cushing had 30 votes and Artemas Ward, Esq., 4 votes for Governor. Charles Cushing, Esq., had 2 votes and Artemas Ward 32 votes for Lieut. Governor.

1787, John Hancock had 43 votes for Governor. Thomas Cushing had 21 votes for Lieut. Governor.

1788, John Hancock had 40 votes and Elbridge Gerry

2 votes for Governor. Nathaniel Gorham had 30 votes and James Warren 8 votes for Lieut. Governor.

1789, John Hancock had 51 votes for Governor. Samuel Adams had 40 votes and Benjamin Lincoln 1 vote for Lieut. Governor.

1790, John Hancock had 45 votes for Governor. Samuel Adams had 44 votes for Lieut. Governor.

1791, John Hancock had 69 votes for Governor. Samuel Adams had 60 votes for Lieut. Governor. Geo. Thatcher, Esq., had 40 votes and William Lithgow, Jr., 24 votes for Federal Representative.*

1792, John Hancock had 55 votes for Governor. Samuel Adams had 41 votes for Lieut. Governor.

1793, John Hancock had 44 votes for Governor. Samuel Adams had 45 votes for Lieut. Governor. Peleg Wadsworth had 52 votes for Representative to Congress.

1794, Samuel Adams had 48 votes and Stephen Pullen 4 votes for Governor. Nathaniel Gorham had 20 votes Moses Gill 5, James Sullivan 3, James Bowdoin 1 and Stephen Pullen 1 vote for Lieut. Governor. Daniel Coney had 42 votes, Dummer Sewall 7, Nathaniel Dummer 9 and Samuel Thompson 30 votes for Senator.

1795, Samuel Adams had 55 votes for Governor. Moses Gill had 57 votes for Lieut. Governor.

1796, Samuel Adams had 59 votes and Increase Sumner, Esq., 85 votes for Governor. Moses Gill had 37 votes and Increase Sumner 15 votes for Lieut. Governor.

1797, James Sullivan had 60 votes, Increase Sumner

*This year the town was divided by the incorporation of Readfield.

15 and Moses Gill 3 votes for Governor. Increase Sumner had 25 votes, Moses Gill 12, James Sullivan 3, Nathaniel Gorham 2 and James Bowdoin 1 vote for Lieut. Governor.

1798, Increase Sumner had 59 votes for Governor. Moses Gill had 29 votes, Thomas Dawes 4 and Thomas Dawes, Jr., 8 votes for Lieut. Governor.

1799, William Heath, Esq., had 60 votes and Increase Sumner 45 votes for Governor. James Bowdoin had 41 votes Moses Gill 36 and William Heath 3 votes for Lieut. Governor.

1800, Caleb Strong, Esq., had 74 votes, Elbridge Gerry 34, Moses Gill 4 and John Blunt 4 votes for Governor.. Nathaniel Wells, Esq., had 60 votes, Moses Gill 11 and William Heath 5 votes for Lieut. Governor. Peleg Wadsworth, Esq., had 22 votes and John Chandler, Esq., 11 votes for Representative to Congress.

1801, Caleb Strong had 77 votes, Elbridge Gerry 3 and Samuel Phillips 2 votes for Governor. Samuel Phillips had 59 votes and William Heath 30 votes for Lieutenant Governor.

1802, Caleb Strong had 70 votes and Elbridge Gerry 22 votes for Governor. Edward H. Robbins had 50 votes and William Heath 20 votes for Lieut. Governor.

1803, C. Strong had 85 votes, C—— Strong 5, Gov. Strong 1, Elbridge Gerry 17, E—— Gerry 46, James Bowdoin 59 and Edward Howard Robbins 95 votes for Governor.

1804, Caleb Strong had 86 votes and James Sullivan 80 votes for Governor. William Heath had 80 votes and Edward H. Robbins 74 votes for Lieut. Governor.

1805, C. Strong had 97 votes and James Sullivan 71 votes for Governor. Edward H. Robbins had 84 votes and William Heath 68 votes for Lieut. Governor. Nathaniel Fairbanks had 91 votes, Nathan Weston 73 and James Bridge 1 vote for Senator.

1806, C. Strong had 117 votes and James Sullivan 63 votes for Governor. Edward H. Robbins had 103 votes, William Heath 64 and James Bridge 1 vote for Lieut. Governor. James Bridge had 103 votes and Thomas Fillebrown 68 votes for Senators.

1807, C. Strong had 112 votes, James Sullivan 67 and Elbridge Gerry 1 vote for Governor. Edward H. Robbins had 105 votes and Levi Lincoln 69 votes for Lieut. Governor.

1808, Christopher Gore, Esq., had 125 votes, James Sullivan 57, William Eaton 5 and David Cobb 2 votes for Governor. David Cobb had 120 votes and Levi Lincoln 55 votes for Lieut. Governor.

1809, C. Gore had 151 votes, Levi Lincoln 56 and John Q. Adams 2 votes for Governor. David Cobb had 142 votes, Levi Lincoln 1 and Joseph B. Varnum 58 votes for Lieut. Governor. Thomas Riel, Esq., had 122 votes, Joshua Cushman 58 and Nathaniel Dummer 24 votes for Senators.

1810, C. Gore had 123 votes and E. Gerry 74 votes for Governor. D. Cobb had 113 votes and William. Gray 73 votes for Lieut. Governor. Samuel S. Wilde had 118 votes and Joshua Cushman 63 votes for Senators.

1811, E. Gerry had 75 votes for Governor. C. Gore had 105 votes, William Phillips 94 and William Gray 76 votes for Lieut. Governor.

1812, C, Strong had 150 votes and E. Gerry 92 votes for Governor. W. Phillips had 149 votes and William King 79 votes for Lieut. Governor.

1813, C. Strong 163 votes and Joseph B. Varnum 75 votes for Governor. W. Phillips had 159 votes and W. King 65 votes for Lieut. Governor.

1814, C. Strong had 150 votes and Samuel Dexter 82 votes for Governor. William Phillips had 136 votes and William Gray 73 votes for Lieut. Governor.

1815, His Excellency Caleb Strong had 153 votes and Samuel Dexter 79 votes for Governor.

1816, Gen. John Brooks had 153 votes and Hon. Samuel Dexter 93 votes for Governor.

1817, His Excellency John Brooks, Esq., had 142 votes and Gen. Henry Dearborn, Esq., 72 votes for Governor.

1818, His Excellency John Brooks had 122 votes and Benjamin Crowningshield, Esq., 59 votes for Governor.

1819, His Excellency John Brooks had 132 votes and Benjamin Crowningshield, Esq., 59 votes for Governor.

1820. This year Maine became a State. Hon. Wm. King had 79 votes, Hon. Samuel S. Wilde 9, Ezekiel Whitman, Esq., 5 and Elijah Davenport 1 vote for Governor.

1821, Hon. Ezekiel Whitman had 95 votes, Hon. Albion K. Parris 31 and John Cushman, Esq., 14 votes for Governor.

1822, Albion K. Parris had 98 votes and Ezekiel Whitman 94 votes for Governor.

1823, Albion K. Parris had 147 votes for Governor.

1824, Albion K. Parris had 123 votes for Governor.

1825, Albion K. Parris had 58 votes and Joshua Cushman 4 votes for Governor.

1826, Enoch Lincoln had 51 votes and Ezekied Whitman 26 votes for Governor.

1827, Enoch Lincoln had 96 votes for Governor. Nathan Cutler had 111 votes, Rev. Joshua Cushman 108, Reuel Williams 99, Sandford Kingsbury 59, Edward Fuller 40 and Joel Wellington 23 votes for Senators.

1832, Daniel Goodenow had 137 votes, Samuel E. Smith 79 and Moses Carlton 22 votes for Governor. Rev. Eliakim Scammon had 240 votes, Jonathan G. Hunton 238, Timothy Boutelle 239, Alfred Marshall 80, Moses Springer, Jr., 79 and Stillman Howard 80 votes for Senators.

1837, Edward Kent had 284 votes and Gorham Parks 93 votes for Governor.

1839, Edward Kent had 201 votes and John Fairfield 107 votes for Governor.

Votes for Governor continued from the preceding page to the present year, 1855.

1840, Edward Kent had 305 votes and John Fairfield 102 votes for Governor.

1841, Edward Kent had 243 votes, John Fairfield 113 Jeremiah Curtis 40 and Scattering 3 votes for Governor.

1842, Edward Robinson had 166 votes, John Fairfield 97, James Appleton 84 and Scattering 2 votes for Governor.

1843, Edward Robinson had 157 votes, Hugh J. Anderson 84, James Appleton 66 and Scattering 13 votes for Governor.

1844, Edward Robinson had 246 votes, Hugh J. Anderson 94, James Appleton 68 and Scattering 1 vote for Governor.

1845, Freeman H. Morse had 171 votes, Hugh J. Anderson 64, Samuel Fessenden 62 and Scattering 3 votes for Governor.

1846, David Bronson had 203 votes, John W. Dana 69, Samuel Fessenden 69 and Scattering 3 votes for Governor.

1847, David Bronson 98 votes, John W. Dana 37, Samuel Fessenden 41 and Scattering 1 vote for Governor.

1848, Elijah L. Hamlin had 136 votes, John W. Dana 60 and Samuel Fessenden 165 votes for Governor.

1849, Elijah L. Hamlin had 145 votes, John Hubbard 59 and Geo. F. Talbot 68 votes for Governor.

1850, William G. Crosby had 159 votes, John Hubbard 83 and Geo. F. Talbot 84 votes for Governor.

1851. No Election.

1852, William G. Crosby had 173 votes, John Hubbard 178, Anson G. Chandler 84 Ezekiel Holmes 20 and Scattering 1 vote for Governor.

1853, William G. Crosby had 160 votes, Albert Pillsbury 111, Ezekiel Holmes 70, Anson P. Morrill 15 and Scattering 1 vote for Governor.

1854, Anson P. Morrill had 217 votes, Isaac Reed 134 and Albion K. Parris 106 votes for Governor.

1855, Anson P. Morrill had 282 votes, Samuel Wells 141, Isaac Reed 94 and Scattering 1 vote for Governor.

CHAPTER V.

Standard of weights and measures—pounds—warning out of town—manufactures—Banks.

"A standard of weights and measures, by order of the Selectmen, were provided for the town by Mr. Benjamin Fairbanks, in the year 1783, and delivered to Nathaniel Fairbanks, Sealer of weights and measures; consisting of 1 half bushel, 1 peck, 1 half peck, 1 gallon, 1 quart, 1 pint, 1 half pint, gill, 1 half gill, 1 ell, 1 yard, 2 pair of scales with steel beams, 1 four pound, 1 two ponud, 1 one pound, 1 two ounce, 1 one ounce, 1 half ounce, 1 quarter of an ounce weight.

Attest: NATHANIEL FAIRBANKS,
Town Clerk."

May, 1789, "Voted to build 2 pounds 30 feet square of sawed timber and cedar posts, one to be set at the east end of Joel Chandler's homestead, the other near the head of the mill pond on Joshua Bean's land, both to be completed by the 1st of May next. Capt. William Whittier bid off the north pound for £2 17s., and with hewn timber if he chose. Amos Stevens bid off the south pound for £2 17s., to be built to the acceptance of the Selectmen for the time being."

A law, requiring the authorities of towns to warn persons, who came into a town to reside without the consent of the town, to depart out of it, began to be put in force in 1789, as follows:

"LINCOLN, SS. To Henry Wyman, Constable of the town of Winthrop, GREETING.

[L. S.] You are, in the name of the Commonwealth of Massachusetts, directed to warn and give notice unto Sarah Follet, in the aforesaid County, the wife of James Follet of Hallowell, who has lately come into this town for the purpose of abiding therein, not having obtained the town's consent therefor, that she depart the limits thereof, with her children, within fifteen days; and of this precept with your doings thereon, you are to make return into the office of the clerk of the town within twenty days next coming, that such further proceedings may be had in the premises as the law directs.

Given under our hand and seal at Winthrop aforesaid, this 12th day of Octo., 1789.

JOHN HUBBARD, } *Selectmen*
SAM'L WOOD, } *of Winthrop.*"

"LINCOLN, SS. Octo. 21, 1789.

This day by virtue of the within warrant, I have given the within named Sarah Follet with her children notice to depart out of the limits of the town of Winthrop within fifteen days, as the law directs.

HENRY WYMAN, *Constable.*

A true copy, Attest: JOHN HUBBARD,
T. Clerk."

The same day, "Catharine Scoot was warned to leave town."

"LINCOLN, SS. To Squier Bishop, Constable of Winthrop, GREETING.

[L. S.] You are, in the name of the Commonwealth of Massachusetts, directed to warn and give notice unto John Clark, Fiddler, a transient person, who has lately come into this town for the purpose of abiding therein, not having obtained the town's consent therefor, that he depart the limits thereof within fifteen days.

Given under our hands this seventh day of Mar., 1792.

NATHANIEL FAIRBANKS, }
SAMUEL WOOD, } *Selectmen.*"

Report says Mr. Bishop once warned a man off of God's earth. Perhaps this was the man; for who has less claim to a dwelling on the earth than a traveling fiddler? The man says, "Where shall I go?" "Go?" says Mr. Bishop, "go to Wayne!"

MANUFACTURES AND MECHANICS.

During the last war with Great Britain, a Copperas mine, near the western shore of the Great Pond, was worked for a season. A very substantial Spruce Yellow was also obtained, with which some buildings were painted. But after the close of the war, the price of copperas became so low, that the works were abandoned.

Messrs. Moses & Charles M. Bailey have an Oil Cloth Carpet Manufactory in the eastern part of the town, where they manufacture and sell annually some $200,000 worth of their goods.

Messrs. Robbins & Hayward erected a building for the manufacture of Oil Cloth Carpeting, to be operated by steam, in 1854, and commenced operations in Jan., 1855.

Messrs. Craigs established a Manufactory for making window-blinds, sashes, &c., in 1854, and are doing considerable in that line.

There have been craftsmen of various kinds from an early period. Mr. Gideon Lambert smote the anvil and first wrought the shoes for their oxen and horses. How long he labored in that vocation is not known. It was not his constant employment; for he cleared up lands and made him a farm. Mr. Moses Chandler was the next blacksmith. Then Mr. John Cole followed the business. In another part of the town, Dea. Benjamin Perkins, and Dea. Luke Perkins and Capt. Asa Fairbanks worked in that line. Very many others, at different times, in several neighborhoods, have been thus occupied.

Col. Nathaniel Fairbanks had a Tannery in the neighborhood of Dea. Metcalf at an early period after the first settlement of the town. He afterwards carried on the business at the village. Mr. Timothy Foster, Jr., practiced the art to some extent in another part of the town. Thomas Eastman, Esq., had a tanning establishment at East Winthrop, where considerable is done in that department. Capt. Samuel Clark has had the largest establishment of the kind, at the village. It is now in the hands of his son, Mr. E. Miller Clark.

The first Shoemaker, was Mr. Ebenezer Davenport, who was also somewhat of a hunter. There are several pretty extensive Boot and Shoe Manufactories. A considerable trade in this line is carried on with California.

Dea. Joseph Metcalf was the first Cabinet and Chair maker. Mr. Charles Robbins and Capt. Samuel Benjamin, who served an apprenticeship with Dea. Metcalf, pursued their trade at the village. Mr. Robbins devoted much time to the study of music, and acquired a respectable acquaintance with its theory. Capt. Benjamin became a skillful workman. He afterwards engaged with Mr. Pitts in constructing horse powers and machines for threshing and cleaning grain. Since the loss of his shop on the stream by fire, he and his sons have erected another near the Railroad station, in which they operate by steam.

Mr. Paul Sears was probably the first Cooper. Dea Charles Harris was of the same craft, in which he continued for many years. His son, Mr. Caleb Harris, followed the business for several years, and then he removed to Mercer. The articles made by the Dea., were of superior workmanship, as were those also of his son.

The House Carpenters have been somewhat numerous. Among the earlier ones were Messrs. Nathaniel Morton, Nathan Howard, Samuel and John Morrill.

Messrs. Adin Stanley and his sons, Lemuel and Morrill Stanley, have been Wagon and Chaise makers. Their carriages are made for durable service.

A Fulling Mill was built upon the stream by Mr. Cyrus Baldwin, in 1791, where the wollen factory now stands. Not long after, he sold to Mr. Benjamin Allen, who sold to Mr. Liberty Stanley and he to Mr. John Cole.

A Blacksmith's shop with a trip hammer was established by Mr. Cole.

Maj. Elijah Wood had a Wrought Iron Nail shop, from which the people for a very considerable distance, were supplied with hammered nails. He employed 20 men. After this, Mr. Samuel Reed manufactured Cut Nails for some years, and then went to Gardiner.

In 1809, the Winthrop Cotton and Wollen Manufactory was incorporated, but did not go into operation till 1814. The building is of brick, eighty feet long, sixty feet wide and four stories high, with a basement for a machine shop. It has a porch which is sixty feet by twenty-three. Their weekly average of cloth is 1500 yards.

Since the removal of Mr. Chandler's mills, a Grist Mill, two Saw Mills, a Wollen Manufactory and two large Shops have been erected, in which Horse Powers, Separators, winnowing machines and various other labor saving machines have been made. These shops were burnt in Feb., 1853. Mr. Luther Whitman has re-built.

In the year 1806, Nathaniel Perley, a lawyer in Hallowell, opened a canal from the North Pond, west of the stream, upon which he erected a Grist Mill, in which, for several years, considerable business was done. But the Cotton Manufacturing Company purchased Mr. Perley's establishment, and closed the canal.

Jonathan Whiting had a Mill on the stream south of his house.

Jedediah Prescot, Esq., had a Saw Mill and a Grist Mill on the stream passing through the Snell farm.

Mr. Squier Bishop was the first Innholder in town. For a succession of years, town meetings were held at his house. His son, Mr. Nathaniel Bishop, succeeded him in the tavern. He erected a store and kept quite an assortment of goods. He afterwards traded many years at the village. Among the other early store keepers, were Mr. John Cole, Maj. Elijah Wood, Capt. Barney Haskell, Mr. Joseph Tinkham and Mr. Samuel Holt.

Mr. John Avery Pitts, a native of this town and an inhabitant until a few years past, at the Paris Exhibition in France, 1855, received the first premium for his Grain Thrasher and Winnower. From the report of the trial of this class of machines, we copy the following statement: "Four thrashing machines were tried, and six men with flails, to test the difference of the labor. Pitt's American thrasher "bore the bell" among them all. The six men thrashed 60 litres of wheat in thirty minutes, Pitt's machine 740 litres, the English machine 410, the French machine 250, the Belgian machine 150. In these trials of reaping and thrashing machines, America stood preëminent, and the effect upon the thousands who witnessed their operations was most happy. The practical and useful character of our inventions is now highly appreciated by the most distinguished men in Europe."

BANKS.

The Winthrop Bank was incorporated in 1824, with a capital of $50,000. As it did not meet the expectation of the Stockholders, after a brief trial, they called in their bills and closed the concern.

The Bank of Winthrop was incorporated in 1853, with a capital of $50,000. That has succeeded so well that $25,000 have since been added. Charles M. Bailey is President, and David Stanley is Cashier.

CHAPTER VI.

Education—schools—graduates—doctors—physicians who have practiced in Winthrop—preachers—lawyers.

EDUCATION.

SOME of the first inhabitants must have had considerable instruction in the common schools. Some of the town clerks wrote a very handsome, legible hand. Their composition was quite respectable. They sometimes violated the rules of syntax. They abounded in the use of capital letters, as the best writers did in those days. Much of their orthography was incorrect. For instance, "Voted to Except a Road three Rods wide." —— were "chosen Committee to enspect The Building of Said house." "Eight o'Clock in the Four Noon." "Notifie — servis — leagul — chuse." Some of them spelled quite correctly.

The young children of the early settlers had very small advantages to obtain an education. But few families came to the place for several years. Some of them had not the means to pay for the instruction of their children. The tradition is, that the first school was taught by Mr. Benjamin Brainerd, in the porch of the house of Mr.

Benjamin Fairbanks. He had about twelve scholars. How long the school continued is not known. This was doubtless more than seventy years ago. Mr. Benjamin Fairbanks was the next school teacher in his own house. Dr. Moses Wing first taught at the Mills, in a room in Mr. John Chandler's house. Mr. Phillip Allen also instructed there at an early period.

The first movement in regard to schools on the town records, is in the warrant for a meeting, March 14, 1774, "to see if the town will hire schooling this year, and how much." The record does not state that the town took any action on the subject. The next mention of the subject is in the warrant for a meeting, March, 1775, "to see how much schooling the town will hire, and what method the town will take respecting the school." In the warrant for a town meeting in March, 1776, was an article relating to schools, upon which they "voted not to raise any money for a school, nor for preaching, nor to defray town charges." The war of the Revolution oppressed them. March, 1777, the article in the warrant "To see if the town will come into some measures to provide a school the year ensuing," was passed in the negative. In March, 1782, the town appropriated twenty pounds for schooling. The Selectmen were authorized to divide the schooling according to their discretion.

The town was divided into six school districts by accepting the report of a committee appointed for the purpose, in December, 1782. In 1783, and in each of the three following years, the town voted to raise thirty pounds, lawful silver money, to support schools. In 1787, they voted to raise fifty pounds, and in 1788 they added ten pounds lawful money to the fifty pounds of the last year.

For a number of years the town chose a School Committee of three in each district, and a Collector of the money for schooling in each district. Generally, but not invariably, one of the Committee was appointed Collector. In 1789, they voted to raise one hundred and sixty pounds to build school houses in the several districts. They appropriated sixty ponnds for schools. 1790, they raised one hundred pounds to hire school teachers, and two hundred and twenty pounds to finish school houses.

April, 1791, Readfield was incorporated into a town.

At the first town meeting after this, Committees were chosen for the several school districts, as follows:

1st district, Benjamin Fairbanks, Timothy Foster and Elijah Fairbanks.

2d district, Stephen Pullen, John Comings and Reuben Brainerd.

3d district, Ebenezer Davenport, Charles Harris and James Atkinson.

4th district, John Chandler, Cyrus Baldwin and Gideon Lambert.

5th district, Phillip Allen, Solomon Stanley and John Fuller.

6th district, Arnold Sweet, Samuel King and Henry Stanley.

1792, thirty-five pounds were raised for the support of schools. In 1793, sixty pounds. In 1794, sixty pounds.

In 1796, three hundred dollars. In 1797, three hundred and thirty-three dollars.

In 1797 or 1798, the interest in having their children instructed, became such, in one district, at least, which is the Snell district, that after expending their portion of the three hundred and thirty-three dollars raised by the town, individuals subscribed two, five or ten dollars each to have the school continued. They were generous enough, not to make it a private school, but allowed al the scholars in the district to attend, whether their parents had subscribed any thing or not. They thus employed a teacher by the name of Burgin, a year and nine months.

In 1800, the town raised four hundred dollars for the support of schools. In 1804, six hundred dollars. In 1807, seven hundred dollars. The same sum was raised annually for many years.

April, 1807, "Samuel Wood, Dudley Todd, Esqrs., Capt, Hushai Thomas and Rev. David Thurston were appointed the School Committee, and were also requested to draw a plan for the instruction of the youth in said town and report at the next town meeting, if they should be of opinion that they can make any improvement of the present plan of schooling."

May, 1807, the committee chosen in April, to report any improvement in the mode of schooling, offered the following:—

"In our opinion, it would be an improvement, if, in all the districts where there are more than 40 scholars, no small children, who cannot read in two syllables so as to be classed with others, should be admitted into the winter schools, and that the teachers in their respective schools should be the judges what scholars are not capable of being thus classed; and in case of any disagreement between the school teachers and parents or guardians of children, it shall be referred to the School Committee to decide.

SAMUEL WOOD,
DAVID THURSTON,
HUSHAI THOMAS,
DUDLEY TODD.

May 4, 1807."

The town accepted the report.

1822, the town voted to raise six hundred and fifty dollars for the support of schools. They continued to raise this sum for the support of schools till 1824, when they raised seven hundred and ninety dollars. In 1825, they raised six hundred and fifty dollars. In 1826, they raised seven hundred dollars. In 1828, they raised eight hundred dollars. They raised this sum annually, till 1833, when the interest on the Ministerial Fund was appropriated to support primary schools, when they raised six hundred and twenty dollars. In 1837, they raised six hundred dollars.

For many years, more than an usual degree of interest was manifested by some of the people of Winthrop to have their schools answer the valuable design of their establishment. The Superintending Committee have been at considerable pains to have the money appropriated to the purpose of education, judiciously expended. Solicitous to have no other than suitably qualified teachers employed, a sense of duty compelled them, occasionally, to withhold the required certificates from applicants. In their visits to the schools, they endeavored to impress upon the minds of the pupils the value of their privileges, and their duty to avail themselves of them in laying a good foundation for an education. They also sought to encourage and stimulate them to be *thorough* in every branch of study to which they attended. Many persons suffer all the way through life from being permitted to pass over their early studies in a superficial manner. Habitually to recite lessons half learned, forms a pernicious habit, which, at length, disqualifies the person for ever doing any thing well.

In their annual reports, which they began quite early to make, the Committee labored to present the responsibility of parents and district agents in selecting suitable instructors for the rising generation. They were earnestly cautioned against the wasteful, insane practice of seeking such as could be obtained for a small compensation. Much stress was laid on having teachers of sound moral principles and correct habits. Parents were urged to indefatigable efforts to have the children make the best use of their time and opportunities. Notwithstanding all the Committee could do, it was sometimes a painful task to make a true report of the state of some schools. The effect, however, on the schools was highly salutary. The Committee had the satisfaction to believe that their arduous and self-denying labors were not lost. Their schools have had the reputation of being better regulated, better instructed, and of having made greater proficiency in their studies than in most other places. They have not unfrequently heard this opinion from competent judges. May they ever maintain a superiority to others in intelligence, morality and every good work.

In addition to the town schools, private schools have been kept for a longer or shorter time, in the district at the village, in that at East Winthrop and in some others. Of late years, they have sometimes had a quarter's schooling in the spring and autumn. A respectable number have gone abroad, to different academies and schools. So that the outlays for education, beyond the legal assessments, have been very considerable.

Rev. John Butler, pastor of the Baptist church in East Winthrop, instructed quite a number of classes of young ladies in the higher branches of an English education. He was a very acceptable and successful teacher. His pupils made highly creditable proficiency in their studies, particularly in Geography and Astronomy. These branches were illustrated by the use of Globes and an Orrery. His school obtained such fame, (nor was it undeserved,) that some of his pupils came from a very considerable distance. His school gave an increased impulse to the cause of female education, not only in this town, but in the region around in various directions.

The whole number of scholars between the ages of four and twenty-one, in May, 1804, was 685. In District No. 1, there were 133; in District No. 2, were 79; in District No. 3, were 102; in District No. 4, were 134; in District No. 5, 39; in District No. 6, were 45; in District No. 7, were 80; in District No. 8, were 31; in District No. 9, were 42. The money raised that year for schools was six hundred dollars.

The whole number of scholars between the ages of

four and twenty-one, in May, 1855, was 777. In District No. 1, 63; No. 2, 76; No. 3, 53; No. 4, 304; No. 5, 79; No. 6, 20; No. 7, 57; No. 8, 48; No. 9, 66; No. 10, 11; No. 11, 4; No. 12, 4.

Winthrop has furnished a large number for the highly important, but by no means duly appreciated, occupation of teaching common schools. Some of them have attained considerable celebrity, not only in Maine and other New England States, but also in the Middle, Southern and Western States.

GRADUATES.

The following is a list of the graduates at different Colleges, from Winthrop.

Abisha Benson, brought up in the family of his uncle, Dr. Peleg Benson, graduated at Dartmouth College, Hanover, N. H., in 1812.

Samuel Johnson, son of Dea. Samuel and Mrs. Susanna Johnson, was born in Rowley, Mass., but came, while a child, in 1802, to Winthrop. He graduated at Bowdoin College in the class of 1817.

George Washington Campbell resided with his brother Daniel Campbell, Esq., and graduated at Union College, Skenectady, N. Y., in 1820.

Samuel Page Benson, youngest son of Dr. Peleg and Mrs. Sally Benson, graduated at Bowdoin College in 1825.

Charles Snell, son of Dr. Issacher and Mrs. Mary Snell, graduated at the same College, the same year.

Samuel Lewis Clark, son of Capt. Samuel and Mrs. Susanna Clark, graduated at Bowdoin College in 1826.

William S. Sewall, son of Rev. Henry and Mrs. Esther Sewall, graduated at Bowdoin College in 1834.

Thomas Newman Lord, after finishing his apprenticeship with his uncle Capt. Thomas Newman, graduated at Bowdoin College in 1835.

Samuel Elliot Benjamin, son of Capt. Samuel and Mrs. Olivia Benjamin, graduated at Bowdoin College in 1839.

William Bradford Snell, son of Capt. Elijah and Mrs. Abba Snell, graduated at Bowdoin College in 1845.

Luther Sampson Gibson, son of Rev. Zechariah and Mrs. Theodate Gibson, graduated at Nassau Hall College, Princeton, N. J.

Perez Southworth, son of Mr. Benjamin and Mrs. Content Southworth, graduated at Bowdoin College in 1846.

George G. Fairbanks, son of Mr. Elijah and Mrs. —— Fairbanks, graduated at Waterville College in 1847.

John Walker May, son of Seth May, Esq., and Mrs. Cynthia, graduated at Bowdoin College in 1852.

Francis Everett Webb, son of Mr. Samuel and Mrs. Olive Webb, graduated at Bowdoin College in 1853, in which he was tutor in Greek one year.

Henry Clay Wood, son of Major Samuel and Mrs. Florena S. Wood, graduated at Bowdoin College in 1854.

DOCTORS.

Winthrop has raised Physicians for several other places.

Bezer Snell, son of Capt. Elijah and Mrs. Abba Snell, went to Virginia in 1818. He was employed as a teacher for some time. He studied the healing art. He went to Red-house, Charlotte County, Virginia, where he has since been in the practice.

John Calvin Metcalf, son of Dea. Joseph and Mrs.

Olive Metcalf, had the degree of M. D., in 1823, from the Medical Institution in Philadelphia. He has been a practitioner in Kentucky since the year 1831.

Gorham Albion Wing, son of Ichabod Wing, Esq., and Mrs. Elizabeth Wing, born July 15, 1798. Having a feeble constitution, his early life was devoted to studies. After he left the town school, he was instructed in Readfield, and was for a season under the tuition of the writer. At the age of fifteen, he commenced teaching a town school. In 1818, he went to Taneytown, Maryland, where he taught school and studied medicine, and after five years he returned, attended Medical Lectures at Brunswick, and in 1824 had the degree of M. D. conferred upon him. He returned to Maryland, and after practicing medicine one year in company with Dr. Hebbard, he removed to Boxborough, Person County, North Carolina for five years. He then went with a company of emigrants to Spring Hill, Maury County, Tennessee, where he remained in his profession, until his decease, May 31, 1854.

Charles Snell, son of Dr. Issachar and Mrs. Mary Snell, had the degree of M. D. conferred on him in 1825, and after practicing some time in Augusta, he went to Bangor, where he still continues the practice.

Samuel Lewis Clark, son of Capt. Samuel and Mrs. Susannah Clark, had the degree of M. D. conferred on him by Jefferson College. Pennsylvania. He had acquired a very respectable degree of skill in the healing art. He practiced some time in Winthrop, but principally in the city of Bangor. He died August, 1851, in the forty-fifth year of his age.

David E. A. Brainerd, son of Mr. Reuben and Mrs.

Fanny Brainerd, received the degree of M. D. at Bowdoin College in 1828. He practices medicine in the town of China.

Nelson Howard Carey, son of Capt. Simeon and Mrs. Roana Carey, had the degree of M. D. conferred on him at Bowdoin College in 1828. He pursued his profession many years in Wayne, and then went to Yarmouth.

George Fillebrown, son of Hon. Thomas and Mrs. Elizabeth Fillebrown, received the degree of M. D. at Bowdoin College in 1831, and at Columbia College, D. C. He pursued his profession in Phippsburg, and secured the confidence of his patients. He died in 1833, aged 39 years.

Josiah Harris, son of Dea. Charles and Melatiah Harris, left Winthrop, April, 1830. He had the degree of M. D. from the Medical College in Baltimore, Maryland. He settled as a physician, in Ohio. For several years, he held the office of Judge in that State, where he yet lives.

Lewis Page Parlin, son of Capt. Silas and Mrs. Mary Parlin, received the degree of M. D. at Bowdoin College in 1834, and pursues his profession in the State of Rhode Island.

Daniel Robbins Bailey, son of Mr. Ezekiel and Mrs. Mary R. Bailey, had the degree of M. D. conferred on him at Philadelphia. He practiced some time at Winthrop village, and then removed to Fairfield. After some years, he returned, and is practising in East Winthrop.

PHYSICIANS WHO HAVE PRACTICED IN WINTHROP.

Dr. Michael Walcott, from Attleborough, Mass., was here about two years, the first regular practitioner in the place, at a very early period. For several years, after he left, the nearest physician was the late Dr. Cony, of Augusta, then Hallowell.

Dr. Moses Wing, from Sandwich, Mass., was some time a physician in town. He married a daughter of Mr. John Chandler, Senior. He afterwards removed to Wayne, where he deceased at an advanced age, July, 1837. He was a member of the Congregational church, and, by the recommendation of some aged ministers, he some times preached to the destitute.

Dr. Peleg Benson was born in Middleborough, Mass., December 14, 1766. He came to Winthrop in 1792. On his way, he taught a school in New Gloucester, and practiced the healing art a short time in Brunswick. November 7, 1793, he married Miss Sally Page, daughter of Col. Simon Page. His early advantages to acquire medical knowledge were very limited, compared with what young men now have. The progress made in the science of chemistry and the establishment of Medical Schools, have rendered very important aid to the profession. Dr. Benson's good common sense and sound judgment secured the confidence of the people. From his experience and observation he acquired a very respectable share of skill and an extensive and successful practice. He was often called by physicians in neighboring towns, as a counselor in difficult cases, particularly in fevers and chronic complaints. He continued the only physician in the place till the year 1806. In 1842, having continued in the profession for half a century, he advertised his friends that he would retire. He died at the good old age of eighty-one years and ten months, October 5, 1848.

In 1806, Dr. Issachar Snell came from North Bridgewater, Mass. He was a graduate of Harvard University of 1797, and had the degree of M. D. conferred upon him, and was M. M. S. Soc. He had given special attention to surgery. He had practiced some prior to his coming to Winthrop. He had performed the difficult operation of Lithotomy with great success. He soon gained practice in town, particularly among the families who emigrated from Bridgewater, of whom there were not a few. His success as a surgeon gave him much celebrity. He was frequently called a very considerable distance in nearly every direction from Winthrop. He became eminent in his profession. To the deep regret of many, he left the town and removed to Augusta in 1828, where he continued in the practice till his very sudden death in October, 1847, aged seventy-two years and five months.

After Dr. Snell left, in 1827, Dr. Charles Hubbard came from Concord, Mass. He had the degree of M. D. conferred upon him, and had enjoyed superior advantages. He was "a well read physician;" but some thought he relied too much on his books. He left in 1830 and went to Lowell, Mass.

Dr. Cyrus Knapp, of Leeds, came to Winthrop in 1827. He received the degree of M. D. from Bowdoin College in 1825. He acquired considerable reputation as a physician. But in 1838, he went to Augusta, and after practicing there some time, he was appointed Superintendent of the Insane Hospital. From thence he went to Rochester, N. Y.

Dr. Ebenezer C. Milliken came from Farmington. The Medical degree of M. D. was conferred on him at Bowdoin College in 1833. He practiced creditably in Winthrop from 1835 to 1837, but was not fond of the profession. He then removed to Boston and went into other business, in which he has been very successful.

Dr. Thomas L. Meguier succeeded Dr. Knapp. He received the degree of M. D. at Bowdoin College in 1827, and came to Winthrop in 1836. He had considerable practice. In 1848 he sold his stand to Dr. John Hartwell, who left in 1854, and has since died.

Dr. Daniel R. Bailey, son of Mr. Ezekiel Bailey, of this town, had the degree of M. D. from the Medical School in Philadelphia. He established himself at the village in 1838, where he practiced some time. He then left, and in 1849 returned and settled in East Winthrop, where he still remains in the practice.

Dr. Samuel Lewis Clark commenced practice here in 1838, and in 1842 went to Bangor and practiced. He was considered a skillful physician. He remained there till about the time of his death.

Dr. Ezekiel Holmes was a native of Kingston, Mass., and a graduate of Brown University, Providence, R. I., in 1821. He had the degree of M. D. at Bowdoin College in 1824. His health not proving adequate to the toils and exposures of a physician, he instructed some time in the Gardiner Lyceum. He came to Winthrop in 1832. In January following, he commenced the publication of the Maine Farmer. He has continued to occupy the Editorial chair of that important and valuable periodical to the present time. He has rendered his weekly issues highly popular and useful to husbandmen and mechanics. He occasionally prescribes as a physician, and not unfrequently is called as a counselor, by the faculty. He was, for 1852 and 1853, the Free Soil candidate for Governor of Maine.

Dr. —— Brown practiced some years in East Winthrop, now Manchester.

Dr. Albert F. Stanley, a native of Attleborough, Mass., received the degree of M. D. at Bowdoin College in 1822, and practiced medicine several years in Dixfield, Oxford County. He came to Winthrop in 1843, where he still continues the practice. He is a cordial laborer in the cause of Temperance.

Dr. Albion P. Snow was a native of Brunswick, where he received the degree of M. D. in 1854. He commenced the practice of medicine in Winthrop, soon after.

Dr. E. Small, a Thompsonian, practiced in 1844, and left in 1845.

Dr. —— Palmer, a Homeopathist, practiced in town in 1852 and 1853, and then removed,

LAWYERS.

The following, who have been admitted to the bar as lawyers, were either born or brought up in Winthrop.

Abisha Benson, a nephew of Dr. Benson, pursued his profession in the town of China. In 1826, he was appointed Brigadier General in the militia. He deceased September 6, 1836, aged thirty-seven years.

Noble Snell, son of Capt. Elijah and Mrs. Abba Snell, practiced law in Virginia.

Samuel Page Benson, son of Dr. Peleg and Mrs. Sally Benson.

Gustavus Adolphus Benson, son of Dr. Peleg and Mrs. Sally Benson.

Seth May, son of Col. John and Mrs. Esther May.

John May, son of Col. John and Mrs. Esther May.

Samuel Elliot Benjamin, son of Capt. Samuel and Mrs. Olivia Benjamin, is practicing in Patten.

William Bradford Snell, son of Capt. Elijah Snell, after being preceptor of Monmouth Academy for some years, has established himself in Fairfield, as an attorney.

Oliver L. Currier, son of Mr. Jonathan and Mrs. Phebe Lambert Currier, was admitted to the bar in Franklin County. He was for some years a member of the Board of Education. He continues his profession in New Sharon.

LAWYERS WHO HAVE PRACTICED IN WINTHROP.

The first regular lawyer in the place was Dudley Todd, Esq. He was a native of Rowley, Mass., and graduated at Dartmouth College in 1795. He came to Winthrop in ——. He was chosen Town Agent in 1801. He served the town in that capacity for a number of years. In 1809, his house was burned, and he sustained a considerable loss, and removed to Portland. But several of his last years, he resided in Wayne.

The next lawyer was Daniel Campbell. He was a native of Chester, N. H., and graduated at Dartmouth College in 1801. He came to Winthrop and opened an office, and in 1837, he went to Readfield, and after practicing some years there, he returned to Winthrop, renounced the law as a profession, and became a preacher.

Alexander Belcher came from Northfield, Mass., to

Winthrop in 1807, where he continued till his very sudden death, in May, 1854, aged 75 years. Though not distinguished as a pleader at the bar, he was well skilled in the principles of law, and was a judicious and able counselor.

Alfred Martin, a native of Hallowell, graduated at Bowdoin College in 1825. He opened an office in 1827. His health declined, and he died in August, 1831, aged twenty-eight years.

Augustus Alden, a native of Middleboro', Mass., graduated at Dartmouth College in 1802. He came to Winthrop, after having been in the profession several years in Norridgewock and Augusta. He removed to Hallowell, where he spent the remainder of his days. He was a pious man, but never had much success as a lawyer.

Jeremiah Lothrop, from Leeds, established himself in the profession in 1828, and subsequently went to Hallowell.

Samuel Page Benson, a native of this town, graduated at Bowdoin College in 1825. After practicing law a while in Unity, came to this town and opened an office in 1829. During the political years 1838 and 1841, he held the office of Secretary of State. In 1853, he was elected a Representative to Congress in the Kennebec or 4th District.

Seth May, a native of this town, practiced law some time in Wayne, and came to Winthrop in 1832, where he still remains. In May, 1855, he was appointed a Judge of the Supreme Judicial Court of Maine.

Thomas J. Burgess, a native of Wayne, commenced the practice of law in this town in 1853.

John Walker May, son of Judge May, was admitted to the bar, August, 1855.

PREACHERS.

Preachers who were members of the Congregational church.

Robert Page, Jr., son of Robert Page, Esq., and Mrs. Abigail Page, graduated at Bowdoin, 1810, and at the Theological Seminary, Andover, in 1815. Though his parents resided in Readfield, yet, they and he were members of the Congregational church in Winthrop. He preached in several places as a Missionary, was ordained pastor of a church in Bradford, N. H., and is now minister in Lempster, N. H.

Samuel Johnson, son of Dea. Samuel and Mrs. Susannah Johnson, was born in Rowley, now Georgetown, Mass. His parents came to Winthrop in 1802. He graduated at Bowdoin College in 1817, and was ordained pastor of the Congregational church in Alna, November 25, 1818. He was dismissed and became pastor of the Congregational church in Saco in 1828. He was appointed Secretary and General Agent of the Maine Missionary Society in 1835. In this vocation he labored till his death, November, 1836. He was a man of popular talents, an evangelical, interesting and useful preacher, cut down in the midst of his days, in the forty-fifth year of his age.

George Washington Campbell, though not a native of Winthrop, yet became an inhabitant. He graduated at Union College, Skenectady, N. Y. in 1823, and was ordained pastor of the Congregational church in South Berwick, November 17, 1824. He has preached in several places since.

Daniel Campbell, a graduate of Dartmouth College in 1801, who had been a lawyer for several years, received the approbation of the Kennebec and Somerset Association as a preacher of the gospel, in May, 1824, and was ordained pastor of the Union church, Kennebunk, Dec., 1827. His health failing him, he was dismissed Dec., 1828. He gradually recovered so much health, that he officiated as pastor of the west church in Orford, N. H., for a number of years, and departed life there in October, 1849, aged seventy years. He was sound in faith and evangelical in spirit.

William May, son of Col. John and Mrs. Esther May, was born November, 1803. He was educated at Bangor, and was of the class of 1827. He was ordained pastor of the Congregational church in Winslow. In Sept., 1833, he was installed pastor of the Congregational church in Strong. Here, July, 1842, he closed his labors and his life. "Blessed are the dead who die in the Lord."

William S. Sewall, son of Rev. Henry and Mrs. Esther Sewall, though not a native of the town, was residing here, and became a student of Bowdoin College, where he graduated in 1834. In September, 1839, he was ordained pastor of the Congregational church in Brownville, where he still continues.

Thomas Newman Lord, born in Newburyport, Mass., August 19, 1807, but brought up in this town, and after closing his apprenticeship, he entered Bowdoin College, where he graduated in 1835. He was ordained pastor of the Congregational church in Topsham, August, 1837. He left Topsham in July, 1842, and was installed pastor of the Second Congregational church in Biddeford, and left, 1853. He is now ministering to the church in Auburn.

Caleb Steadman Williams, son of Mr. John and Mrs. Eunice Williams, became a Licentiate for the ministry, but has not been ordained.

Luther Sampson Gibson, son of Rev. Zechariah and Mrs. Theodate Gibson, graduated at Nassau Hall College, Princeton, N. J., was Licensed by Presbytery. He was an Agent of the American Sunday School Union, and died while in their employ.

Samuel N. Tufts, son of Mr. Samuel and Mrs. Sally Tufts, received the approbation of the Union Association, as a candidate for the ministry, September, 1843.

Perez Southworth, son of Mr. Benjamin and Mrs. Content Southworth, graduated at Bowdoin College in 1846, and after spending some time in the Theological Seminary at Bangor, he received approbation to preach. He went to the South for the benefit of his health, and preached a few weeks in Georgia. In passing through Tennessee on his way to Kentucky, he died of cholera, June 15, 1849, in the 27th year of his age. A mysterious dispensation of God's providence, it appears to us. He was a youth of fair promise, had struggled hard to qualify himself to be useful in the vineyard of the Lord, and was thus suddenly cut down in the morning of life.

Francis Southworth and Alanson Southworth, sons of Mr. Benjamin and Mrs. Content Southworth, are members of the Bangor Theological Seminary, in the course of preparation for the ministry.

CHAPTER VII.

Ecclesiastical History — Meeting Houses — Congregationalists — Friends—Methodists—Calvinist Baptists—Universalists—Christian Band—Free Will Baptists—Ministerial Fund.

ECCLESIASTICAL HISTORY.

A REVIEW of the past may be made instructive and useful. God repeatedly enjoined it upon his people to "call to remembrance the former days." Many have found it interesting and profitable. "He established a testimony in Jacob and appointed a law in Israel, which he commanded our fathers that they should make known to their children the wonderful works that he had done, that the generation to come might know them, even the children which should be born; who should arise and declare them to their children, that they might set their hope in God, and not forget the works of God, but keep his commandments." Ps. 78 : 4—7. So the devout Psalmist, 77 : 10, 11, said, "I will remember the years of the right hand of the most High, I will remember the works of the Lord, surely I will remember thy wonders of old." The history of the past, judiciously reviewed, may afford valuable materials for humiliation, admonition, warning, direction and encouragement.

The glorious Redeemer said to his disciples, "Ye are the salt of the earth; ye are the light of the world." Matt. 5: 13. He therefore scatters his people into different portions of the land, to preserve the inhabitants from moral darkness and corruption. What preacher of the gospel first proclaimed the glad tidings of salvation to the inhabitants of Winthrop, the writer has not ascertained. The early settlers had been accustomed to attend upon the institutions of the gospel. They could not fail to perceive that they and their families needed to feel the benign influences which accompany those institutions. They soon began to make arrangements to have the gospel preached among them. But what measures were taken, prior to the incorporation of the town, in 1771, to have the ministrations of the gospel, I have not been able to learn. But, on the 27th of May, 1771, in a legal town meeting, "John Chandler, Timothy Foster and Jonathan Whiting, were appointed a committee to hire preaching for eight Sabbaths the ensuing summer; and to raise twenty pounds, to hire preaching and defray other necessary charges." Who was employed, if any one, the records do not show, but it was probably Mr. Thurston Whiting. The town annually chose a committee to hire preaching for two or three months. Mr. Whiting had preached considerably to the people prior to October, 1775. The town then "instructed their committee to agree with him for three months, after his other engagements are out, and to hire him one day in a month during this winter, with a view of settling him." The instructions some times given to the committee, were, "to hire a young gentleman of good moral character." There were special reasons for such instructions. For the Province of Maine was the "city of refuge" to which ministers of unsound morals, generally fled.

March 11, 1776, they "voted not to raise any money for preaching," or for schools, or to defray town charges. The reason doubtless was, the embarrassment which the war occasioned. But they "voted to employ Mr. Moore* to get Mr. Thayer to preach in this town four Sabbaths.

About this time, some of the inhabitants began to have scruples in regard to raising money by tax, to pay for preaching. The town, September 9, 1776, "voted to dismiss Micajah Dudley, Stephen Dudley, Jabez Clough, Moses Ayer, Benjamin Fairbanks, Timothy Foster, Jr., Stephen Norton, Daniel Dudley, from paying any ministerial charges in this town," on account of these scruples. "Voted to meet at the nearest convenient place in the center of the town for public worship, and that we meet half of the time at the house of Mr. Henry Wyman, and the other half of the time at the house of Mr. Squier Bishop, till the committee can fix upon a place in the center. Voted to hire Mr. Jeremiah Shaw four Sabbaths more than what the committee have agreed with him for. Voted to raise £20 lawful money, to defray ministerial charges. Voted to Mr. Jeremiah Shaw four shillings, which he paid for a pilot through the woods."

No records can be found from which it can be ascertained how much preaching the people had enjoyed prior to this time. It is inferred, that Mr. Shaw had preached there a considerable time, from the fact, that the town "voted to Mr. Jonathan Whiting for Mr. Shaw's board,

* Probably Mr. Moore of Pownalborough.

£2 14s., and for keeping Mr. Shaw's horse, 12s. No mention is made of what was paid the minister.

Several persons had come into the place, who were members of churches in Massachusetts and New Hampshire. They, with some others, who had not made a public profession of religion, were desirous of enjoying the special ordinances of the gospel. Accordingly, they requested an Ecclesiastical Council, composed of the churches in Harpswell, Pownalborough* and New Castle, to convene for the purpose, should it be judged advisable, to organize a church. In compliance with this request, Rev. Samuel Eaton of Harpswell, Rev. Thomas Moore of Pownalborough, and Rev. Thurston Whiting of New Castle, assembled in Council, Sept. 4, 1776. Whether Delegates were present is not known, as the record of the Council is lost. But members of the church have told me that after the examination of the candidates, and they had subscribed a covenant, embracing articles of faith and practice, the Council declared the covenanters, (26 in number,) to be a church of Christ.†

Mr. Shaw was probably preaching here when the Congregational church was organized. On the 22d of that month, the church extended an invitation to him to become their pastor. On the 7th of October, the town "voted to give a call to him to settle in the ministerial office; and to give him £60 lawful money salary for the first five years, and then to add £15 to his salary, during his public administration among them. Also to give him 200 acres of land in the nearest convenient place, in the

* Now Dresden, or Wiscasset, for Pownalborough included both.

† See Appendix, Note D.

center of the town, that can be obtained. Mr. Ichabod How, Mr. John Chandler and Mr. Joseph Baker, were chosen a committee to wait on Mr. Shaw, and to present him with the proceedings of this day." But he declined accepting their proposals.*

Jan. 15, 1777, a committee was appointed to "hire a young gentleman to preach three months, that can be well recommended as a preacher, and as to his moral character; and that the committee invite the neighboring ministers to preach one day apiece with us this winter, *gratis*." They also agreed to "reward Rev. Mr. Emerson for one day's preaching last winter, and Mr. Whiting for one day's preaching last summer.

October 13, 1777, the church and town extended a *unanimous* invitation to Mr. Zaccheus Colby, a young preacher, to become their pastor. The town "voted to give Mr Colby eighty pounds per annum for his salary during his ministry, stated at corn 4s. per bushel, rye at 5s., and beef at 5d. per pound, and what money he receives towards his salary shall be in proportion to the aforesaid articles as herein stated. And to prevent all misunderstanding of this vote, it is the true intent and meaning of the same that, if said articles should fall, that said salary should fall in proportion, but that his salary shall be paid in proportion to the above articles, not exceeding the within price." Captains Timothy Foster and Ichabod How and Mr. Stephen Pullen were the committee to present these proposals of the town to Mr. Colby. "Voted

* Mr. Shaw was afterwards many years pastor of the church in Moultonborough, N. H.

to raise fifty dollars to pay for preaching and the expenses of getting Mr. Colby down here." He also returned a negative answer to their call.

Mr. Colby graduated at Dartmouth College in 1777.* In 1811, he told the writer, that his youth and inexperience induced him to decline accepting their invitation. No one is able now to say what portion of the time they were favored with the ministrations of the gospel.

March 9, 1778, a committee was appointed to provide preaching, and also March 8, 1779. This committee were instructed "to write Mr. Colby not to preach here unless he concluded to settle here; and not to employ any gentleman as a preacher, unless on probation of one, two or three months, as they may think best, and a man well recommended."

May 17, 1779, "Voted to divide the town into two Parishes by an East and West line to pass in the center, as lately found by the town committee."

March 18, 1780, the town "voted to raise six hundred and twenty dollars to pay Mr. Sweat, and his board and horse keeping." Who this Mr. Sweat was, is not known. Probably he had been preaching on probation, but for reasons now not known, did not become their pastor.

They still remained like "sheep scattered upon the mountains without a shepherd." They had to contend not only with the difficulties and hardships incident to all who establish themselves in newly settled countries, but some privations and trials which were peculiarly griev-

* Mr. Colby was many years pastor of the church in Pembroke New Hampshire.

ous. Surrounded by an immense wilderness, far from the habitations of civilized men, they were subjected to many serious inconveniences. The Revolutionary war prevented intercommunication by water, (nearly their only way,) with the older settlements at the West. This greatly enhanced their troubles. Still, they were not wholly deserted and cast off. Through the good hand of God upon them, they were brought to more prosperous days.

October 17th, 1781, Rev. David Jewett, who had been pastor of a church in Candia, N. H., was invited to become their pastor. The 19th of November, he signified his acceptance of their proposals.* The same day, the church and the pastor elect, agreed to send to the following pastors and churches, viz.: Rev. Messrs. Upham of ———, Chadwick of Scarboro', Webster of Arundel, (now Biddeford,) Eaton of Harpswell, Whiting of New Castle, and Moore of Pownalborough, to compose the installing Council. January 2, 1782, the installation took place. But who of them attended and performed on the occasion, is not known. The result of the Council is lost.

In about fourteen months after the installation, their pastor was removed by a very sudden death. Thus they were left again without a spiritual guide. During the long period of seventeen years, they remained destitute of a pastor, and much of the time, of the regular ministrations of the gospel. It was no marvel, that in such a

* See Appendix, Note E.

state, they should have to encounter many, various and sore trials. Internal dissensions rent them. When the soothing, benign influences of the preached word are removed, what else is to be expected? If, when churches are favored with all the salutary appliances of the gospel, the members should disagree, is it strange that, when they are withdrawn, they should have strife and envying? Some of them dishonored their profession, by their unchristian spirit and practice. Other denominations made inroads upon them. Some removed to a distance. Others were called to go the way of all the earth. Their number was reduced and their strength weakened.

They were not left utterly desolate, nor without some intervals of light and refreshing. A portion of the time they had the faithful preaching of the gospel. The ministers in all the region were few. Rev. Ezekiel Emerson of Georgetown, now Phippsburg, and Rev. Samuel Eaton of Harpswell, occasionally visited them, to advise, counsel and encourage them, and brake unto them the bread of life. They would spend a Sabbath and considerable part of the week with this feeble, destitute, afflicted church.

August 14, 1786, the town voted to hire Mr. Jacob Cram, a graduate of Dartmouth College in 1782, who had been preaching with them some time, six weeks longer; and that he preach half of the time in the north part of the town, and to raise ten pounds to pay him. They also voted to build a porch over the front door of the meeting house. On the 22d of September, they gave Mr. Cram a call to the work of the ministry, "by a large majority;"

and for a salary, they agreed to give him one hundred and twenty-five pounds, to be paid in produce, Indian corn at 4s. per bushel, rye at 5s., beef at 3d. per pound. Gideon Lambert, Jonathan Whiting, Robert Page, Esq., Benjamin Brainerd, William Pullen, Simon Page and Elijah Fairbanks were appointed a committee to present the invitation of the town to Mr. Cram.

He also returned a negative answer to the call of the town.* Why it was, that so many preachers declined settling in this town, is not easy to explain. They certainly needed a pastor.

April, 1787, "the town voted not to choose a committee to provide preaching." They allowed "Nathaniel Fairbanks' account for boarding Mr. Cram last year, £4 1s."

January 14, 1788, Jonathan Whiting's account was allowed of £13 3s. 7d., which he paid to Rev. Mr. Sweat, for preaching.

In the warrant for a meeting of the town, March 24, 1788, the "5th article was to see if the town will employ Mr. Eliphalet Smith, or some other man, to preach with us this year; which passed in the negative."

May 5, "Voted, that Capt. John Blunt, Doct. John Hubbard and John Chandler, Jr., be a committee to procure some labor done on the Ministerial Lot; and instructed them not to clear nor to employ men to clear more than 50 acres, and not to rent said land for more than 10 years; and to have said land cleared as reasonably as in their power."

August 27, 1788, they declined taking measures to have preaching.

* Mr. Cram was afterwards settled in Hopkinton, N. H.

Rev. David Jewett had presented a large folio volume, containing the works of Rev. Mr. Flavel, to the people in Winthrop. At the town meeting, March, 1790, "voted that Capt. Fairbanks take care of said Book."

September 6, 1790, "Voted to raise sixty pounds to hire preaching. Voted that each man who shall wish to be exempted from the above sum, shall make his plea, and that the town vote them clear or not, as they shall think proper. Voted to exempt Jabez Clough, Benjamin Fairbanks, Daniel Marrow, James Craig, Paul Sears, Samuel Stevens, Steuart Foster, John Gray, Timothy Foster, David Foster, Daniel Wing, Peter Norton and Joshua Bean." Jonathan Whiting, Esq., Capt. Solomon Stanley and Jedediah Prescot, Jr., were a committee for the south part of the town; and Capt. William Whittier, Robert Page, Esq., and Dr. John Hubbard for the north part of the town, to lay out the above sum of money to hire preaching.

March, 1791, the town was divided, and the northern part incorporated by the name of Readfield.* The Legislature of Massachusetts subsequently authorized the town to sell the land given by the Plymouth Company for the support of the ministry in the town of Winthrop, and to divide the proceeds of the sale between the two towns, and to appropriate the interest of the money for the support of the ministry.

The Ecclesiastical history from this period pertains to Winthrop alone. Hitherto, Readfield has been included.

* See act of incorporation, in the Appendix, Note F.

April 4, 1791, "Voted, that £40 be raised to hire preaching, to be laid out by the Selectmen, or a committee chosen for that purpose." May 9, 1791, Amos Stevens, Jedediah Prescot, Jr., and Capt. Nathaniel Fairbanks were chosen a committee to hire preaching.

May, 1792, the town voted not to apply to Mr. Atkinson to preach any longer in this town.

May, 1793, they agreed to raise thirty pounds to hire preaching.

April, 1797, they voted not to raise money to have the ministrations of the gospel.

May, 1798, "Voted to raise one hundred dollars to hire preaching;" which money they voted to have assessed, collected and paid in to the town Treasurer in six months. Jedediah Prescot, Esq., Elijah Fairbanks and Amos Stevens were chosen to appropriate the money, with discretionary orders, only, the town voted that they should "pay none of said money to any person as a preacher, unless there was a probability of his becoming the settled minister of said town."

September, 1798, they voted not to employ Mr. Steele any longer. There are no means of knowing how long they had employed him, nor why they did not wish to retain him.*

September, 1798, they decided not to hire Mr. Jotham Sewall, or any other candidate, to preach among them.

May, 1799, voted not to raise any money for preaching.

* It is believed that this Mr. Steele was afterwards settled at Machias.

December 30, upon the article in the warrant, "whether the town have any objection to the incorporation of a Society in said town, (at the next session of the General Court,) to be known by the name of a Religious Congregational Society, for the purpose of supporting public worship in that order." "The town voted *unanimously*, that they had no objection to the incorporation of said Society, at the next session of the General Court."

From November, 1781 till 1800, during this period of nineteen years, seventeen of which the church had no pastor, no record of any act of the church, nor of any baptism, can be found. The Clerk told me that he kept an account of the transactions; and when a pastor was ordained, he transferred the records to him. This was a season of great moral darkness and gloom. Religion declined; iniquities abounded. The Sabbath was grossly profaned. What part of the time they had preaching, cannot be correctly ascertained. But all "the salt had not wholly lost its savor." Some were truly grieved for the desolations of Zion. Some of the more considerate persons, without the pale of the church, became alarmed at the prevalence of impiety and vice. Convinced of the enlightening and reforming tendency of the ministrations of the gospel, they were desirous to have its institutions among them. The Christians felt a very tender solicitude for the spiritual welfare of the rising generation. They saw them coming forward on the stage of life, uninfluenced by those means which God has appointed for the conversion and salvation of men. "They wept and made supplication," they besought God "to behold and visit this vine." He, who, in faithfulness chastens his people, but never utterly forsakes them, heard their supplications. The clouds of thick darkness, which had long hung over them, began to disperse. A brightening, gladdening prospect opened before them. But so various were the views of the inhabitants of the town on religious subjects, and so divided, that they could not act as a town in the settlement and support of a minister.

Several men, though not members of the church, were decided and substantial friends of religious institutions and order, in connection with members of the church, obtained from the Legislature an act of incorporation, *as a Poll Parish.** They could then act in a legal way to raise money to support religious worship.

In the winter of 1799 and 1800, Mr. Jonathan Belden, from Weathersfield, Conn., a graduate of Yale College in 1796, and a candidate for the gospel ministry, came among them. His labors were attended by the special influences of the Holy Spirit. The season was memorable, and numbers will retain a very grateful remembrance of it through eternal ages. From this period the cause of evangelical religion asssumed a new and brighter aspect in the place.

In May, 1800, the church *unanimously* invited Mr. Belden to become their pastor. The Parish concurred in the invitation. On the 27th of August following, he was ordained their pastor.† But the pastor's health became impaired and at the expiration of five years, Sept. 10, 1805, an Ecclesiastical Council "unanimously advised that the pastoral connection between the Pastor and

* See the act of incorporation—Appendix, Note G.

† See Appendix, Note H.

church be dissolved in compliance with his and their wishes."

In 1806, the Poll Parish was dissolved by an act of the Legislature. The writer, having been invited to preach a few Sabbaths in the place, came in the beginning of May, that year.

In June, the church kept a day of fasting and prayer in reference to a meeting of the town to be held on the 11th, to see whether they would raise money to support preaching.

The town met and "voted to raise two hundred and fifty dollars for the purpose of supporting a preacher of the gospel. Nathaniel Fairbanks, Nathaniel Kimball and Isaac Smith, were appointed a committee to appropriate the above sum." They engaged the writer to supply the pulpit. Nov. 10, the church having previously extended an invitation to him to become their pastor, the town "voted to give him a call to settle in said town in the work of a gospel minister; and to give him four hundred dollars a year, so long as he shall continue our minister; and also voted to give him four hundred dollars as a settlement, to wit: one hundred dollars yearly, if he should continue our minister for the space of four years, if he should not, then his settlement to decrease in proportion to that time, and so in that proportion until the four years have expired." Samuel Wood, Esq., Dea. Elijah Snell and Mr. Jonathan Whiting, Jr., were chosen to present the proposals of the town to Mr. Thurston.

In January, 1807, Mr. Thurston returned an affirmative answer to their invitation to become their minister;

and was ordained their Pastor, Feb. 18, 1807.* The pastoral relation continued until Oct. 15, 1851, when, at his request, it was dissolved in accordance with the advice of an Ecclesiastical Council. During his pastorate 327 were added to the church. The same day Rev. Mr. Thurston was dismissed, the Rev. Rufus M. Sawyer was ordained their Pastor.*

The first Sabbath School in town and propably in the State, was established by this church, Aug. 7, 1808. It has been continued in different forms, and with various success, until the present time. The number in the Sabbath School is one hundred. They have renewed their Sabbath School Library several times and it now contains three hundred volumes.

FRIENDS.

A few individuals, residing in the Easterly part of the town, embraced the principles, and adopted the language, costume and habits of the Friends. Twelve heads of families and some twenty-five of their children were organized into a Society, according to the usage of their Denomination, in 1792. The following composed the meeting at that time, viz. Steuart Foster and wife, David Foster, Ephraim Stevens, and wife, Samuel Stevens and wife, (of Readfield) Daniel Robbins and wife, Josiah French and wife and Moses Wadsworth. They erected a house of worship in their neighborhood in 1798. Not long after this Ezra Briggs and wife came into the place from Dresden and united with them. The children of

* See Appendix, Note H.

Steuart and David Foster did not remain with the Friends, nor did some of the other children. Several removed to other places. They built a second house of worship in 1843 and a larger one in 1853. Their present number, including children is about seventy. In this little society are some very enterprising young men. They have gone extensively into the Oil cloth carpet manufacture.

EPISCOPAL METHODISTS.

There was a Methodist class formed in the S. E. part of the Town in what is called the Fairbanks' neighborhood, in 1794, under the ministrations of Rev. Philip Wager. Of what number the class consisted cannot now be ascertained. Nathaniel Bishop, and Seth Delano were probably the only men. The wives of S. Delano, Nathan Richmond and Daniel Marrow, were probably the females.

In 1806, 7 and 8, the Methodists preached in the school house in that neighborhood once in two weeks. Subsequently they preached there but seldom. A Methodist minister had, occasionally, preached in the Village, but not at stated times, till 1825. Mr. Nathaniel Bishop and his wife had been, for many years, members of that communion. He had formerly been a local preacher. From the date last named, he made great efforts to introduce local preachers from the neighboring towns.

He projected the plan of having a Methodist Chapel erected in the Village. The plan was opposed very considerably, but being a man of indomitable perseverance, he succeeded. He and several others obtained a very eligible site, and on the "24th of June, 1825, the corner stone was laid; and after the frame was raised, but being yet uncovered, on July 3d, Bishop Soule preached within it." At the annual meeting of the Maine Conference at Gardiner, the following week, Winthrop was considered a station, but no preacher was appointed till the next annual Conference. Local preachers, however, regularly preached on the Sabbath. The chapel was completely finished and solemnly dedicated to the worship of Almighty God, November 23, 1825. Rev. Stephen Lovell preached on the occasion from 2. Chron. 7: 15, 16. In July, 1826, the Conference appointed him to take charge of this station. The number belonging to the class at this station then was *twenty-one*, only fifteen of whom were members of the church.*

In 1854, the number of members in the church was reported to be one hundred and four, and eight on probation. The officers and teachers in their Sabbath school numbered nineteen, their scholars were one hundred and twenty, and their Sabbath school Library contains 270 volumes.

CALVINIST BAPTIST CHURCH.

From an early period in the history of Winthrop, there were some of this donomination in the easterly part of the town. They were connected with others in Readfield; and in 1792, were organized into a church, then called the Baptist church in Winthrop. But having erected a house of worship in the eastern part of Read-

* See Appendix, Note I.

field, they changed the name to "the Baptist church in Readfield."

In April, 1794, after the outside of the town meeting house was finished, the town voted that the Baptists might occupy the house two Sabbaths out of five. Whether they availed themselves of this offer, I can not say. Rev. Abraham Cummings did preach some time in the place, prior to 1800. He was an open Communionists and often supplied Congregational churches. Whether he preached for the Baptists, *particularly*, or for the people of the town, is not known. It does not appear from the records that he was ever employed by the town.

In 1809, the Baptists asked the town for their share of the money, for which the land given by the Plymouth Company for the support of the ministry, had been sold; but the town voted not to grant it. They occasionally had preaching in the school house in the east part of Winthrop, on the Sabbath and other days.

In the summer of 1823, they erected a house of worship, which was solemnly dedicated to the worship of God the Father, Son and Holy Ghost, November 19, 1823. The sermon was preached by Rev. Stephen Chapin, Professor in Waterville College, and was published. Mr. Phinehas Bond, a licentiate, preached among them with much success.

June 22, 1824, a church was organized by an Ecclesiastical Council, composed of the following Elders and Delegates: Elder D. Chessman, Dea. James Hinckley and Brother William Cross, Hallowell; Elder John Haines, Brothers Joseph Anderson, Abijah Crane and

Jeremiah Richards, Fayette; Brothers Asa Axdell and Ebenezer Gilman, Belgrade. Elder Titcomb of Brunswick, Dr. Chapin of Waterville, Elder Nutter of Livermore, Elder Wilson of Topsham, Elder Butler and Professor Briggs of Waterville, and Brothers Phinehas Bond and Ezra Going, licensed preachers, being present, were invited to sit with the Council, and take part in the proceedings.

Thirty persons, eighteen males and twelve females, members of the Baptist church in Readfield, but residing in Winthrop, were dismissed to be constituted the First Baptist Church in Winthrop. (See Appendix, Note K.)

June 28, *twenty-four* males and *forty-one* females were received by letters from the church in Readfield. Several had been baptized, and July 11, 1824, seventy-four were added to the church, twenty-seven males and forty-seven females. August 8, twelve more were added to their number, four males and eight females. At the close of that memorable year, the church consisted of *one hundred and twenty-nine* members, of whom fifty-one were males.

Their first pastor, Rev. John Butler, was installed May 1, 1825; and continued about *seven* years. He was succeeded by Rev. Samuel Fogg.

February 23, 1836, Rev. John H. Ingraham was ordained pastor of the Baptist churches in East Winthrop and Hallowell X Roads, (now Manchester.) April 13, 1839, at his request, his pastoral labors among them ceased.

From September, 1839, Rev. Daniel E. Burbank ministered to them, till his health failed, and he deceased,

October 26, 1840, aged twenty-three years. Cut down in the morning of his days, and in prospect of extensive usefulness.

October 23, 1840, Rev. Franklin Merriam was ordained their pastor.* He continued their minister till some time in 1848.

January 24, 1849, Rev. Sampson Powers was ordained their pastor.* He remained pastor till the latter part of 1852.

Rev. C. W. Bradbury was their last minister. They have no settled minister now.

Rev. George G. Fairbanks, a member of this church and graduate of Waterville College, is now pastor of a Baptist church in Somerville, Mass.

The number of scholars in the Sabbath School, at the close of 1854, was one hundred. Their Sabbath School Library contains 575 volumes.

UNIVERSALISTS.

Who first preached or professed to believe, that all men would be finally saved in this place, may now be difficult to decide. A preacher, by the name of Barnes, occasionally, came from Poland and taught that sentiment. At his meetings at the school house at the Mills, a number attended, among whom, at times, it has been said, there was no female. They did not have stated ministrations, until the year 1819. "A preliminary meeting was held December 4, 1818 to consider the propriety of having a minister. On the 31st of March, 1818, Messrs. Moses Johnson, John Morrill, Jacob Nelson, and

* See Appendix, Note K.

thirty-eight others formed themselves into a Society denominated the Union Society in the towns of Winthrop' Readfield and Wayne." This Society was organized into a corporate body according to the laws of Mass. They employed a minister by the name of Mace, who preached in the three towns. A part of the time, they had preaching in this town half of the time, sometimes less and sometimes more. They were supplied by different ministers. This state of things generally, remained, till their number had increased, so that August 26, 1837, they organized a Society in this Town. In the Preamble to their Constitution, they say, "We, the subscribers, feeling desirous to grow in grace and in the knowledge of our Lord and Saviour Jesus Christ, do hereby form ourselves into a Society that we may be helps to each other and that, by our united energies, we may better serve the purpose of religion and faith, we cheerfully accept and subscribe the following constitution.

ART. 1. This Society shall be called the first Universalist Society in Winthrop.

ART. 2. The object of this Society shall be the promotion of truth and morality among its members, and also in the world at large; and as the gospel of the Lord Jesus Christ is calculated above all other truth to inspire the heart with emotions of benevolence and virtue, this Society shall deem it one of its main objects to support the preaching of the gospel according to the society's ability, and to aid in any other proper way of spreading it among men.

ART. 3. Any person sustaining a good moral character may be admitted a member of this Society, on application to that effect, by a majority of votes at any regular meeting.

ART. 4. It shall be regarded the duty of every member to adorn the doctrine of the Lord Jesus Christ with a well ordered life and conversation; to contribute according to his ability, in the manner determined on by a majority, towards the support of public worship and other necessary expenses of the society; to attend upon the exercises of the sanctuary, as well as the regular meetings of the society for businses. A habitual neglect of any of these duties shall be regarded sufficient reason for striking the name of any member from the roll by a vote of the majority."

The other articles provide for meetings of the society, choice of officers, their duties &c.

About *fifty* men have signed this constitution, some *twenty* of whom have either deceased, removed, or left the society. Many others have been voted in as members, who have not subscribed the constitution. Between 1836 and 1838, Rev. G. Quinby ministered to them.

In the summer of 1838, they erected a very neat and commodious house of worship, opposite the Methodist Chapel in the western part of the village. This house was dedicated December 25, the same year, on which occasion Rev. Mr. Gardiner of Waterville preached. Rev. Giles Bailey came Sept. 1839. At his ordination, Rev. Mr. Willis of Mass. preached. A church was organized near that time consisting of eighteen members. *

*See Appendix, Note L.

Mr. Bailey continued with them until the autumn of 1842. Rev. Frederic Foster, a native of Haverhill, Mass., and graduate of Dartmouth College of 1840, was ordained pastor in 1842, and remained about two years.

Rev. Geo. W. Bates preached with them all the time during one year, commencing in 1846. Rev. D. T. Stevens succeeded Mr. Bates, and supplied them more than a year.

Their present minister, Rev. O. H. Johnson, began his labors among them in 1853. They have a Sabbath school of one hundred and thirteen members, and a Sabbath school library of 400 volumes.

CHRISTIAN BAND CHURCH.

Several persons in the south west part of Winthrop, united with the Christian Band. They had a house of worship just beyond the bounds of this town in Monmouth. But that house has been removed and become a dwelling house.

FREE WILL BAPTISTS.

The Free Will Baptists in Winthrop and Wayne, erected a house of worship on the line between the two towns. They worshipped there a few years. But in consequence of erecting a house of worship at Wayne village, the one first named was deserted and has since been removed.

HOUSES FOR WORSHIP.

The subject of erecting a house for the public worship of God, had been agitated at different times, but no effective measures had been taken to accomplish so important and desirable an object. But at their annual meeting in March, 1774, they appointed "Joseph Baker, Ichabod How and John Chandler, a committee to build a house for public worship, 36 feet long and 30 feet wide, and to set it on lot 57,* in the nearest convenient place to the center of the town on said lot."

At a town meeting, July 28, 1774, "Voted, that the committee to build the meeting house shall take money of the town rates sufficient to buy nails and glass for the house. Voted that the common hands that work on said house be allowed 3s. 4d. per day, if they find themselves." "This house was glazed, but never finished inside or outside."†

October 19, 1775, Jonathan Whiting, Joseph Stevens and John Chandler were "a committee to effect the finishing of the meeting house; and that this committee enclose the lot on which the meeting house is built, as soon as may be."

"November 5, 1781, the town was divided into two parts for public worship, as the water divides it, the south pond, so called, the mill stream, the mill pond and from the most northerly part of the mill pond, a north line to the end of the town. So long as we remain one commonwealth, the preaching is to be in equal halves on both sides of the town." They agreed to build two houses for worship. "Voted, that the east meeting house shall be built on the County road, near Lieut. Abraham Wyman's; and that the dimensions shall be, 55 feet long, 45 feet wide and 24 feet posts. That the

* This is the lot on which Mr. M. Haven Metcalf now lives.

† Letter of Noah Prescot, Esq.

west meeting house shall be built on the height of land between Ebenezer Davenport's and James Work's, on the side of the Town road; and that the dimensions shall be, 50 feet long, 48 feet wide and 23 feet posts. Voted, that Jonathan Whiting, Benjamin Brainerd, Samuel Foster, Josiah French and Squier Bishop shall be a committee for the east side of the town; and Solomon Stanley, Amos Stevens, James Work, James Atkinson and James Craig shall be a committee for the west side of the town." Each of these committees was "instructed to provide materials for building as fast as they can." "Voted to assess £100 hard money, to be paid in money, on the east side of the town, to procure nails and glass; and to assess £400 on the east side of the town to be paid in labor, or materials for building. Voted to assess £80 hard money, to be paid in money, on the west side of the town, to procure nails and glass; and £320 to provide timber for the frame, underpinning, boards and shingles, and people are to have liberty to work if they will." Neither of these houses was built.

At the meeting the 21st of January, 1782, a proposal was made to re-consider the votes passed for dividing the town into east and west divisions, and for erecting two houses of worship, which did not prevail. They voted, however, to repair the old meeting house "so as to be comfortable to meet in for a number of years." At a meeting, March 11, "Voted to grant £30 lawful money, to be laid out in repairing the meeting house, at the best discretion of the committee," who were James Craig, Jonathan Whiting and William Pullen.

November 21, 1782, "Voted to move the meeting for

public worship from the meeting house to Mr. Chandler's and Mr. Whiting's the ensuing winter, every other Sabbath at each place, in case the inhabitants in the north-east part of the town do not desire one-sixth part of the preaching, if they do, it is granted them; likewise the north-west part of the town is granted one-sixth part of the preaching, in case they desire it."

January 10, 1785, they "Voted again to divide the town into two Parishes, by an east and west line, so that the north part shall be about four miles wide and the south part about five miles." William Pullen, Joshua Bean and Samuel Foster were chosen a committee to sell the meeting house. This they probably did, to David Woodcock.*

May 13, 1786, "Voted that David Woodcock's note for the meeting house be given up, and that he return the nails of the old meeting house to the town."

At a meeting, May 8, 1786, the town voted to build two meeting houses, the south, on a spot between David Woodcock's and William Pullen's. Solomon Stanley, Squier Bishop and Nathaniel Fairbanks were appointed a committee for building this house. William Whittier, Josiah Mitchell and Robert Page, Esq., were chosen a committee for building the north house. They also agreed to raise four hundred pounds lawful money, to be expended in building both houses.

July 3, the town voted to "build the north meeting house on lot No. 136, between the highway and the south

* Some of the timber of the old meeting house is said to be now in the cider mill of Mr. Columbus Fairbanks.

line of said lot, about 70 or 80 rods west of Samuel Taylor's house."

At a meeting, June 12, Amos Stevens and Daniel Marrow were added to the committee for building the south meeting house; and it was decided that the house be fifty by forty feet. The Selectmen were to procure a convenient site for the house. The committee were instructed to procure timber for the house, and to proceed immediately to frame and raise it; and to give the people opportunity to work and find such materials for the house as they could most easily provide; and that they should use, as far as practicable, the productions of the country in erecting the house.

"May 9, 1791, voted to raise one hundred pounds to finish the outside of the meeting house, and to build a porch over the front door. Capt. Solomon Stanley, Amos Stevens and Benjamin Fairbanks were chosen a committee for this purpose."

May, 1792, fifty pounds were raised towards finishing the meeting house.

At the town meeting, April, 1794, the committee appointed to finish the outside of the meeting house, reported that they had accomplished the object of their appointment, and the report was accepted by the town. The town, at this meeting, "voted that the Baptists may have the improvement of the meeting house two Sabbaths out of five, and to begin to occupy it the third Sabbath from this date."*

April, 1800, "the town voted to dispose of the meeting house to the first Congregational Society, on conditions,

* This is the house which, for some years past, has been used as the Town House.

that said Society will finish said house in such a term of time as shall be agreed on by a committee this day appointed by the town, viz: Jedediah Prescot, John Comings and William Richards, and by a committee to be appointed by said Society, and selling the pew ground to any persons in said town of Winthrop, who shall choose to purchase, at public auction. The town reserving to themselves the privilege of said house for a Town House; provided said Society will give as much for said house, (if any thing,) as three disinterested men, viz: John Hubbard, Esq., Capt. John Evans and Robert Page, Esq., shall judge they ought, taking into view every circumstance." They then chose Benjamin Fairbanks and Nathaniel Fairbanks a committee "to represent the circumstances relating to the meeting house to the above referees."

At the meeting of the town, May 5, the committee appointed to say what the town should receive as compensation for their meeting house, should it be conveyed to the first Congregational Society in said town, "having examined said house, do report that, the town shall convey said house to said Society upon conditions that said Society shall finish said house and continue to keep it in good repair for the use of said town, as expressed in the vote passed at the April meeting, so long as they shall continue a Society; and if they shall be dissolved as a Society, the house which shall then be standing, shall revert to the town, as their exclusive property.

JOHN HUBBARD,
JOHN EVANS, } *Committee.*
ROBERT PAGE,

Winthrop, May 2, 1800."

"The town voted to accept this report on condition that the said Society will reserve four pews, or seats to that amount, on the lower floor, and as many in the galleries, in proportion to the bigness of the floor, for the use of the town: said pews or seats to be in as eligible a situation as the pews or seats are, take them together."

The house was finished, and although the first Congregational Parish was dissolved by an act of the General Court of Massachusetts, in 1806, yet the Congregational Society continued to occupy the house until August 7, 1825. A solemn and affecting farewell was taken of the house, as a place of worship, in a discourse from Deut. 8: 2. There, nearly forty years, the people of God had been accustomed to assemble to attend on his worship and ordinances, to humble themselves before him, to supplicate his mercy and celebrate his praise. Taking leave of a place, around which so many hallowed associations clustered, could not fail to awaken strong emotions. Numerous reminiscences of the most touching and interesting character were called up. Few were the bosoms which did not swell and eyes which did not freely weep.

The first Parish had erected a house,* decent in appearance, commodious in size and structure, convenient in location, in which to celebrate divine worship. Three days after bidding adieu to the old house they met in the new one, and, with appropriate religious services, solemnly dedicated it to Jehovah, Father, Son and Holy Ghost.

On that occasion, however, the gladness and joy of

* That which they now occupy.

having succeeded in obtaining what had been ardently desired, were mingled with very mournful and distressing recollections of what occurred at raising the frame of the building in which they were then convened. On the *ninth* of June, 1824, a numerous company was gathered. There was no intemperance, profaneness or noise. The calmness, harmony, dispatch and success, which attended the enterprise, until more than half the rafters were in their places, were unusual. One spirit of cheerful anticipation appeared to animate the whole company of active laborers, and spectators. But suddenly the scene was changed. A beam broke, the shoring not being sufficient, and from thirty to forty men, mingled with a ton or two of timber, were precipitated a distance of *twenty-six feet!* It seemed almost miraculous that half of them were not killed upon the spot. Yet, some were scarcely hurt, others slightly, some seriously, and three mortally wounded. But the scene beggars description. The lamentations of neighbor for suffering neighbor, of brother for suffering brother, of children for father, of fathers for sons, of wives for husbands, were enough to melt the heart. But the groans of the wounded and dying, were truly agonizing. One, who had been married not two full months, laid speechless and unconscious for a few hours, and yelded up the ghost.* Another, lingered in a state of excruciating distress till about noon the following day, and died, leaving his afflicted widow overwhelmed with grief.† Another, for whose recovery considerable

* Warren Pullen.

† Paul Ladd.

hope was entertained, on the morning of the third day after the fearful catastrophe, exhibited symptoms which awakened the most alarming apprehensions among his sorrow smitten friends. Before the going down of the sun, the lamp of life was extinguished.* Thus another widow and three fatherless children were added to the group of unexpected and distressed mourners. "Shall there be evil in the city and the Lord hath not done it?" Amos 3 : 6. "Be still and know that I am God." Psalm 46 : 10.

MINISTERIAL FUND.

It does not appear that the town took any action in regard to the lot of land given by the Plymouth Company for the use of the ministry in Winthrop, after the incorporation of Readfield into a town, until their meeting in November, 1798, when they "voted to instruct Col. Fairbanks, their agent, to confer with the select men of Readfield, who are concerned, and if they and the town of Readfield consent, to apply to the general Court for leave to sell it." This they did, and obtained an act of the general Court, Feb. 18, 1799. The sale amounted to $1576,60. the proportion which Winthrop received was $840, 85. As they had no settled minister at that time, the money was loaned and the interest added to the principal until about 1816.

It will be observed that for some years the town had granted no money to sustain the institutions of the gospel among them. From 1806, when they began again to raise money for this purpose by a *tax*, several individuals

* Francis Hoyt.

were dissatisfied. They did not wish to pay their money to aid in the inculcation of religious sentiments, which they did not believe. Leading men in the town maintained, that a tax could not be legally assessed and collected, unless all liable to be taxed were assessed. The town were willing all, who desired to be exempted from being taxed, should be, provided they would take measures to be legally exempted, as they all might be.

May 1798, the town voted to raise one hundred dollars to hire preaching and to have it " assessed, collected and paid in to the town treasurer in six months. Jedediah Prescot Esq., Elijah Fairbanks and Amos Stevens were chosen to appropriate the money." 1799, voted not to raise any.

" Jan. 20, 1800, the town remitted the ministerial tax voted in 1798 in the bills of Moses Joy collector, to the following persons agreeably to their desire viz. Benjamin Fairbanks, William Richards, Samuel Foster, Joel White, Seth Delano, Asa Robbins, Paul Sears, Ephraim Stevens, Moses Wadsworth, Daniel Robbins Jr., David Foster, Josiah French, Steuart Foster, Aaron Wadsworth."*

Accordingly, at a meeting of the town, Jan. 8, 1810, " they voted, that Nathaniel Bishop, Benjamin Fairbanks, Seth Delano, Elijah Fairbanks, Daniel Foster, Benjamin Fairbanks, Jr., Elijah Fairbanks, Jr., Asa Robbins, Enos Fairbanks, Eleazar Robbins, Rial Stanley, Nathan F. Cobb, and Thomas Jacobs, may be incorporated into a regular Society by the name of the Methodist Society in Winthrop." At a meeting, the 5th of Feb. they voted " not to grant liberty to the Methodist Society to poll to and from the said society." The town declined acting

* Town records.

on the request of the Methodist "for their proportion of the ministerial fund given for the support of the ministry."

Feburary 1811, the Methodists in town were incorporated into a society, and according to the laws of Massachusetts, the remaining inhabitants, as regards ecclesiastical concerns, were the successors of the town and denominated the First Parish.* In this capacity, they claimed the ministerial fund. In 1816, "the First Parish" proposed to pay the interest of the ministerial fund towards the salary of the minister. Many thought this would be a perversion of the money, as there were other denominations in town, who claimed equal right to a share of the fund to support their ministers. The fund now amounted to $2837.34.

This fund now became a source of very unhappy contention. The Parish sued the town and in 1819, obtained a decision of the Supreme Court of Massachusetts, that the fund belonged to them. But some law questions remained unsettled, until Maine became a separate State in 1820. The case was then brought before the Supreme Court of Maine, and they decided in the same way. But that did not settle the difficulty. Many of the inhabitants believed they had a moral right to their portion of the income of the fund.

In Feburary 1832, the Parish, in order to allay the unhappy dissentions which had so long prevailed, agreed to yield up the ministerial fund to the town, on the condition that the interest arising from the fund should be annually appropriated to the support of the town schools, provided, an act of the Legislature be obtained giving authority thus to appropriate it. This was done, and thus the contention has ceased.

---

* See the act in Appendix Note I.

CHAPTER VIII.

Morals—The Winthrop Society for the promotion of good morals —Temperance—Efforts made by the town to effect a reformation of morals—Temperance tavern—Sons of Temperance—Watchman's Club—Anti-Slavery—Society for Mutual Improvement—Agricultural Societies—Kennebec Agricultural Society —Literary Societies—Anderson Institution—Franklin Society —Lyceums.

MORALS.

"SIN is a reproach to any people." The state of morals in a community goes far towards determining the degree of estimation in which they are entitled to be held. A people free from vicious principles and practices deserves to stand higher than one, in which a laxness of moral principles and practice prevails. A morality, based on the principles of the gospel, gives respectability and worth to any place.

During the first half of the present century, from 1800 to about 1850, the people of Winthrop were distinguished for the general prevalence of sound morality. If their morals were not as corrupt as some others, they certainly were not as pure as desirable. Individuals began to feel impressed with the duty of making more direct and energetic efforts to stay the progress of vice than had been made. The preservation and improvement of morals in a community have ever formed an object of high importance in the estimation of all wise and good men. At a time when vice prevails to such a degree, as justly to occasion grief and alarm to all considerate persons, it is especially incumbent upon the friends of order and piety to combine their efforts to arrest its progress. Convinced of the present need of reformation, and believing that a righteous God will succeed suitable measures for the prevention of evils alike destructive of domestic and social enjoyment and of the eternal welfare of men, and for the promotion of good morals, a number of persons in Winthrop deemed it advisable that a society should be formed for the purpose of attempting to effect a reformation of morals among us. Articles proposed as the basis of a Constitution had been signed by upwards of forty persons, and previous notice having been given, a meeting of the subscribers was held, March 27, 1815, for the purpose of organizing a society, which was styled

THE WINTHROP SOCIETY FOR THE PROMOTION OF GOOD MORALS.*

The following were elected officers of the society, viz.

SAMUEL WOOD, Esq., *President.*

Rev. ZECHARIAH GIBSON, *Cor. Sect'y.*

---

* See Appendix Note M.

Rev. DAVID THURSTON, *Recording Secretary.*
Mr. DANIEL HAYWARD, *Treasurer.*

Rev. ROBERT LOW,
Dea. CHARLES HARRIS,
Mr. SAMUEL THING, } *Committee.*
Dea. JOSEPH METCALF,
Mr. CHARLES ROBBINS,

Resolved, That we highly approve the efforts which are making by various Associations in our country to arrest the progress of vice and raise the morals of our fellow citizens, and that we pledge them, particularly the "Massachusetts Society for suppressing intemperance" our sincere and cordial coöperation.

Resolved, That we will afford our encouragement and aid to the tithingmen in this town, that they may be enabled, with greater effect, discreetly and faithfully to discharge the difficult duties of their office."

The Recording Secretary was requested "to procure fifteen copies of the Pamphlet, published by the Middlesex Convention, to promote the better observance of the Lord's day, for the use of the tithingmen in this town." At a meeting of the Society, October 2, 1815, "the Standing Committee were requested to procure 500 copies of a printed Address to be distributed among the youth of this town, upon the duty and importance of more generally attending public worship on the Lord's day."

TEMPERANCE.

Dram drinking in stores was becoming an appalling evil. At the meeting of the Society March 25, 1816, the Standing Committee were instructed to take such meas-

7*

ures as their discretion might dictate, to prevent the evils resulting from the present mode of retailing spirituous liquors at the stores. In September the society instructed their committee to circulate the Address of President Appleton, D. D., delivered before the Massachusetts Society for suppressing intemperance, particularly among the members of this society; and to take such other measures as they shall deem expedient to awaken the public mind to the importance of reform in regard to the manner of retailing spirituous liquors. At the meeting in October, the use of spirituous liquors was discussed and after the reading of a very interesting circular addressed by the committee of the Bedford Society for the suppression of vice, to the venders of spirituous liquors, it was

Resolved, that this society view the use of spirituous liquors, except as a medicine, or in some rare cases, as injurious, and that in the present state of things, civility does not require and expediency does not permit their being used as a part of hospitable entertainment in social visits. ***Passed unanimously.***

Much pains were taken by personal interviews with the store keepers and by printed addresses, to prevail on them to desist from the practice of dealing out drams to "be drunken in and about their shops," and they were distinctly told, that unless they ceased this dreadful work of making drunkards, it was "the fixed determination of the society to have the law regulating the sale of spirituous liquors *strictly enforced.*"

At the meeting of the society, March 1817, "a committee was appointed to consult the Supreme Judicial Court, as to the best mode of preventing the sale of ardent spirits by the small quantity, i. e. by the glass, or gill, as practiced by the storekeepers in this Town and County."

At the meeting in October following, the committee reported that they had been unsuccessful in their labors with the storekeepers. Rev. Mr. Gillet of Hallowell preached a very appropriate discourse before the society from James 5 : 20. Various plans were devised to prevent the fearful evils of intemperance by endeavoring to prevail on men to use intoxicating drinks *only moderately*. But just as long as moderate drinking was countenanced, not a few would become drunkards.

In March 1818, the society altered their constitution, so as to embrace the establishment and patronage of Sabbath Schools as a means of promoting correct morals. At the same meeting the society resolved to attempt to establish a Sabbath school in each school district in town. Rev. Mr. Tappan of Augusta was invited to deliver a discourse before the society at the next semi-annual meeting. But for some reason, he did not. At the meeting in September it was stated, that " in seven districts, Sabbath schools had been commenced and continued for different periods and with various success ; but in all, with so much as to afford encouragement for future exertion."

In April, 1819, a law had been recently passed, making it a penal offence to furnish intemperate persons with spirituous liquors, gratis or otherwise ; and " every vender of spirituous liquors, who shall permit any minor, tipler, common drunkard, or gambler to remain in his house or store, or any part thereof, exposes himself to a fine of ten dollars in addition to the forfeiture of former laws; and if he furnish any such person with any kind of strong drink, he forfeits his license and the privilege of having it renewed again for three years."

The selectmen were authorized to post the names of common drunkards in all public places in town where spirituous liquors were sold, forbidding the venders to sell to any such person.* The society requested the selectmen to post two individuals, after giving them notice that they should do it, if they persisted in their present habits. The selectmen did not post either of them, " as one of them had not frequented the stores as formerly and the other had been more regular." From this date, the principal efforts of the society were directed to the organizing and maintaining of Sabbath schools, till the close of 1832, when the society was discontinued. The churches had adopted the institution as one of their instrumentalities.

EFFORTS MADE BY THE TOWN TO EFFECT A REFORMATION OF MORALS.

At a meeting of the town, April 6, 1830, they "voted to accept the following Preamble and Resolve, offered by Samuel Wood, Esq.:

WHEREAS, This is an age of reformation in regard to the unnecessary use of *distilled spirits*, and inasmuch as towns in their corporate capacity should do something to check the progress of this alarming evil, some efforts having been made by individuals of this town to ascertain

---

* See Appendix Note M.

the quantity which has been annually retailed in the village in this town, (exclusive of Innholders,) and it appearing from an investigation of the subject, by an actual reference to the bills of the merchants, who have kindly and willingly furnished the information needed, with the exception of one, who declined, for reasons best known to himself; but the quantity which he sold being estimated during the time he sold, on an average with the other merchants; that the enormous quantity vended in said village, in six years, commencing January 1, 1824, and ending January 1, 1830, amounts to 23,159 1-4 gallons, which, estimating West India rum at $1,10, New England rum at 42 cents, gin at $1,25, and brandy at $1,60 per gallon, which is calculated to be their average price during said time, amounts to the consumers to no less a sum than $19,541,09, or annually, $3,260,18; and on the supposition that one half of it was consumed by the inhabitants of this town, it is believed to be a very low estimate, there having been, generally, during said time, one store in the west part of the town and another in the east, and many of the inhabitants of this town obtaining their supplies from other towns, it will appear that the inhabitants of this town have paid annually for the articles above named, an amount of money but little short of all their other money taxes, during the same term; and the town of Winthrop has always been considered a temperate town. Notwithstanding this is undoubtedly true, as to a very large portion of the inhabitants, yet there is an alarming evil stalking among us, which is believed to be caused in no small degree by licensing so many to retail spirits by small quantities, which renders it thus easily obtained; and inasmuch as we are desirous of lessening the effects of this serious evil, and are also desirous, for the benefit of the present and rising generations, that our deliberate opinion on this subject may be entered on the records of this town; therefore,

Resolved, That the use of ardent spirits, in health, or as a part of social entertainment, is a heavy and unnecessary tax on the community and destructive to the morals of society, and that it is not our duty as a town to tempt men to use it by licensing any individuals, except Innholders, to sell it to be drunk in their stores or shops, and that we will not recommend to the officers of this town to do it, or pass any vote authorizing such a measure."

December, 1832, the town "instructed the Selectmen and town Agent to discountenance the violation of the law in relation to the sale of ardent spirits, and to take proper measures to prevent the violation of said law in future, and also to carry into effect the law with regard to posting drunkards and tipplers."

April, 1836, "Voted not to license any person to sell ardent spirits in town the ensuing year in a less quantity than twenty-eight gallons; and that the town Agent be directed to prosecute all violations of the license law."

Several other temperance societies have been formed. Very many sermons, addresses, and lectures have been given, in which the appalling evils resulting from the use of intoxicating liquors have been faithfully portrayed. The sinfulness of indulging that morbid appetite has been shown. The constitution of the first society organized on the principles or Total Abstinence from all intoxicating beverages is not to be found. It was adopted early in the progress of the reform and a very respectable number kept the pledge.

TEMPERANCE TAVERN.

The first tavern, on the principle of total abstinence in the town, if not in the State, or the country, was kept by Dea. Daniel Carr. This was a thorough total abstinence house. It was not like many others, having out the sign of Temperance, but still keeping the means of making drunkards in some obscure part of their house. Many travelers were in the habit of saying, that there was no tavern, in which they could not obtain intoxicating drinks. But they could never find it at Dea. Carr's, for the very substantial reason, that it was not there.

WASHINGTONIAN SOCIETY.

The Washingtonian Society was formed October 15, 1841. The first officers were,

JAMES C. HOWARD, *President,*

WADSWORTH FOSTER,
LORING FOSS,
CALVIN RICHARDSON, } *Vice Presidents.*

ROBERT L. JACKSON, *Secretary,*

DAVID STANLY, *Treasurer,*

EXECUTIVE COMMITTEE.

S. Lewis Clark,	Moses Joy.
Lingan Curtis,	John Dorsett,
E. P. Stevens,	John O. Wing,

Ezra Whitman, Jr.

SONS OF TEMPERANCE.

The Sons of Temperance, under the title of United Brothers, Division No. 44, were organized October 16, 1846. Their whole number was 88. They paid to sick members during their existence $214,00.

WATCHMAN'S CLUB.

In the winter of 1850 a Watchman's Club, No. 71 of the Order, was formed. This organization was commenced in Durham in this State, in the spring of 1849. The specific object of this association was, to procure the enactment of a stringent prohibitory law against the sale of intoxicating liquors.

The Legislature for 1851 was elected mainly upon the temperance issue, and in the course of the session they enacted a law for the suppression of "drinking houses and tippling shops." This enactment embodied some principles of organic law, which had never before been applied to the temperance cause. It produced a great sensation in this State and in other States, and thus came to be denominated the "Maine Law." This Law greatly encouraged the hearts of temperance reformers, and sent confusion into the tents of the traffickers. The Watchmen thus early having obtained the object of their desire, now zealously embraced this law and determined to see that it was thoroughly executed. This was no part of the duty of "Divisions" in their associated capacity, and as it was not judged necessary to have two organizations for a similar purpose, the Division was dissolved, May 23, 1851, that they might add strength to the Club. "Moral suasion," had been tried, till its power was well nigh exhausted. The necessity for a judicious and faithful execution of the *Law* became constantly more apparent. The Club set themselves in earnest to stop the nefarious traffic and not without effect.

There have also been organized a Marth Washington Society—a Division of the Daughters of Temperance, or the Band, The Union Temperance Society, and a Juvenile Temperance Society. All of them have rendered valuable aid to the cause of temperance.

It is a matter of just lamentation and deep grief, that after all these efforts, a drunkard, or the means of making one, should be found in the place. To what a depth of depravity that individual must have reached, what a perfect wreck of all the sympathies of our common humanity must he have made, who at this day, in this place, for the paltry gains of rumselling, will continue to gratify the morbid appetite of the inebriate, injure his health, destroy the domestic peace of the family, demoralize his character, ruin his reputation and thus facilitate his progress to the drunkard's grave and the drunkard's eternity. What employment does so effectually steel men's hearts to such a degree, as the liquor traffic? The squalid poverty, the wretchedness, the tears, the agonizing entreaties of wives and children occasioned by it, cannot prevail on those engaged in it to desist.

ANTI-SLAVERY.

The first Anti-slavery sermons, showing the inherent sinfulness of slaveholding in the United States, and the duty of immediate emancipation, were preached by the pastor of the Congregational church, November 21, 1833.

An Anti-slavery Society was organized, on the principle of immediate abolition, embracing *one hundred and seven* members, March 4, 1834. The officers were,

Rev. DAVID THURSTON, *President*,
Dea. JOSEPH METCALF, } *Vice Presidents*,
Dr. EZEKIEL HOLMES, }
Mr. STEPHEN SEWALL, *Secretary*,
Mr. SAMUEL CORDIS, *Treasurer*.

The Society, at their meetings, which all were invited to attend, discussed the subject. For they held it as a sacred, invaluable right, that men might freely discuss any subject, involving the principles of morality, or the innate right of men, as men, to "life, liberty and the pursuit of happiness." They purchased and distributed books and tracts on the subject. They established an Anti-slavery Library, and observed the monthly concert of prayer for the enslaved.

A Female Anti-slavery Society did worthily for the cause of the oppressed, by their instructions and contributions.

A Juvenile Anti-slavery Society had been organized, and was addressed, March 29, 1838. The object of the Society was to inform them in regard to the character of slavery, that they might be convinced of its sinfulness, so as never to become slaveholders, or be the apologists of a system fraught with such dire evils. By reading the "Slaves Friend," and other publications on the subject, they would imbibe such views and receive such impressions that would tend powerfully to prevent their becoming slaveholders. If all the young, in the New England States even, had been suitably instructed and trained on the subject of human rights, slavery would have lost one of its principal supports.

SOCIETY FOR MUTUAL IMPOVEMENT.*

Although this Society was not confined to Winthrop, yet a report of the first Directress to Mrs. Tappan, then Secretary, will give some idea of what the females in Winthrop were then doing for benevolent purposes. The report is therefore given. The following were the officers of the Society for the year 1837.

1st. *Directress*, Mrs. DAVID THURSTON, Winthrop.
2d. *Directress*, Mrs. BENJAMIN TAPPAN, Augusta.
Sec. and Treasurer, Mrs. THOMAS ADAMS, Waterville.

WINTHROP, JUNE 22, 1837.

My dear Mrs. Tappan :—In compliance with the provisions of the Constitution of the Society for Mutual Improvement, I have the satisfaction to report, that our Maternal Association embraces among its members the greater part of the mothers in the *church*.† Our meetings were held once in two weeks, and, during the past year, have been attended with a good degree of punctuality. A few cases of hopeful conversion have taken

* See Appendix Note N.

† The object of the Association was to assist mothers to a better understanding and more efficient performance of their highly responsible duties. For this purpose, they met, consulted and prayed together.

place within the year in the families of some of the mothers. There is also a female prayer meeting attended every other week, quite as numerously attended the past year, and with as much, if not more, interest, than in former years.

The female Moral Reform Society now numbers about one hundred members. It embraces females of different denominations. The meetings have been kept up once a fortnight without any abatement in interest. Several copies of the Advocate of Moral Reform are taken by the Society for the purpose of distribution. A degree of assurance is felt that the society is exerting a considerable influence of a very salutary character.

A female Anti-Slavery Society has been recently organized, including some of different denominations, which promises to be a valuable auxiliary in delivering from that degrading, soul-destroying system, by which more than a million of our sisters are enslaved. This society is calling forth an increased sympathy for those of our sex in this land, who have no protection for their persons, their reputation or their virtue.

A sewing circle, composed of young ladies who meet once in two weeks, has been kept up with a good degree of interest. They appropriate the avails of their labor to various benevolent objects ; and have accomplished as much, if not more than in any preceding year.

We have also a female juvenile society which meets once in three weeks. These meetings are attended by two members of the church, one of whom reads, while the other superintends the work. They devote the avails of their labor to some charitable object. One prominent design of the meeting is to have the members early acquire the habit of doing good.

I had been making my arrangements and fondly anticipating the pleasure of meeting my beloved sisters at the approaching anniversaries, but the providence of our heavenly Father calls me to remain at home to watch over the sick. Grateful for the respect shown me in placing me first on the list of officers, I am constrained to request, sincerely and earnestly, that some other may be appointed as first Directress.

Praying that you may enjoy the presence and blessing of the Lord Jesus Christ, I am your affectionate sister,

P. B. THURSTON."

MORAL REFORM SOCIETY.

The reading of McDowell's Journal, which he began to publish in the city of New York, in 1833, awakened the attention of several of the good women in Winthrop, to the prevalent, soul-destroying sin of lewdness. Their sympathies were aroused. The dangers to which the purity of their own children was exposed, were presented in a new and alarming light. They met, prayed, consulted, and, in 1833, formed the "Female Moral Reform Society." Besides contributing directly to the Parent Society, they paid for several copies of the Journal, while that was published, and then for a larger number of the "Advocate of Moral Reform," which they distributed. Notwithstanding the odium attempted to be cast upon these efforts, they have been productive of immense good to the cause of moral purity.

8

Several other Societies, in different neighborhoods, for the promotion of objects of benevolence, have been organized. Missionary Associations have rendered important aid in providing the means of salvation for the destitute. These efforts have had a very wholesome influence upon the members. To practice self-denial for the sake of doing good to others, directly counteracts the native selfishness of the heart. It expands the soul and prepares men to devise liberal things.

If the people of Winthrop have not been renowned for their public spirit and large heartedness, some of them have been liberal and have done well for the various objects of benevolence. To what good cause have they not contributed ? To what benevolent enterprize have they not lent their aid ? The funds of the Bible Society, the Education, Misssionary, domestic and foreign, the Tract, Moral Reform, Anti-Slavery and Temperance Societies have all been increased by their donations. That they have done as much as they should is not pretended. But if the people in all other towns had done as much in proportion to their means as those, who have contributed in Winthrop, the treasuries of our eleemosynary institutions would have been far better replenished than they have been.

AGRICULTURAL SOCIETIES.

Prior to 1818, a Society had been organized with a view to improve the art of husbandry and to elevate the calling of the husbandman. Not a few of the young men were beginning to look upon farming as rather a low employment. They were aspiring to something higher. Appearing to forget, that this was the original employment of man, and that those, in all other occupations are sustained by it, they were disposed to hold the tillers of the soil as not in a very honorable position. "The profit of the earth is for all; the king himself is served by the field." Ecclesiastes 5: 9. The efforts of the Society gave such promise of success, that they obtained an act of incorporation from the Legislature of Mass., February 21, 1818. Alexander Belcher, Peleg Benson, David Foster, Charles Harris, Dean Howard, Nathan Howard, Joseph Metcalf, Issachar Snell, Joseph Tinkham, Enoch Wood, Elijah Wood and Samuel Wood, were the corporators. The first meeting under this act was held, July 4, 1818. The officers then chosen, were,

SAMUEL WOOD, *President*,
NEHEMIAH PIERCE, *Vice President*,
JOSEPH METCALF, *Corresponding Secretary*,
ALEXANDER BELCHER, *Treasurer*,
DAVID THURSTON,
PELEG BENSON,
ISSACHAR SNELL,
JOSEPH NORRIS,
DAVID FOSTER, } *Trustees.*

At the annual meeting, March 7, 1832, that the Society might conform to an act then recently passed by the Legislature of Maine, the name was changed to that of the

KENNEBEC AGRICULTURAL SOCIETY.

The officers for that year, were,

SAMUEL WOOD, *President*,
GEORGE W. STANLEY, *Vice President*,
ELIJAH WOOD, *Corresponding Secretary*,

SAMUEL BENJAMIN, *Recording Secretary*,
SAMUEL CHANDLER, *Treasurer*,
WILLIAM C. FULLER, *Collector*,
SAMUEL P. BENSON, ELIJAH WOOD, NATHAN FOSTER, } *Trustees.*

The efforts of the Society to improve the art of husbandry were very successful. Some of the most skilful cultivators of the soil among us entered into the subject with a zeal and perseverance which gave a new impulse to the important and noble cause. They were accustomed to assign tasks, or experiments, to individuals, in order to ascertain what kind of soils was best adapted to specific crops. Divers experiments were tried, and their results were reported and discussed at the meetings of the Society. Thus, much valuable, practical information was gained, which gave considerable celebrity to the farmers in Winthrop. The Trustees made annual reports in writing. Some of these were elaborate productions, which, through the press, found their way to many a husbandman, beyond the limits of the town. The influence of this Society was felt in the adjacent towns; and contributed not a little towards the formation of other Societies, particularly, the North and South Kennebec Agricultural Societies. It also had an influence in the establishment of kindred Societies in other portions of the State. It prepared the way for the introduction of the Annual Exhibition of Agricultural and Horticultural products, of improvements in the implements of husbandry, and the "cattle shows." On all these occasions, they were accustomed to have a public address, which generally, was printed in newspapers or pamphlets. The present officers, chosen Feb. 7, 1855, are,

FRANCIS FULLER, Winthrop, *President*,
HOWARD B. LOVEJOY, Fayette, *1st Vice Pres.*,
JOHN MAY, Winthrop, *2d Vice President*,
OAKES HOWARD, Winthrop, *3d Vice President*,
DAVID CARGILL, Winthrop, *Record'g Secretary*,
EZEKIEL HOLMES, Winthrop, *Cor. Secretary*,
RUSSEL EATON, Augusta, *Treas'r & Librarian*,
DANIEL A. FAIRBANKS, Augusta,
S. H. RICHARDSON, Readfield, } *Trustees.*
DANIEL TRUE, Wayne,
S. N. WATSON, Fayette, *Agent & Collector.*

The Society is prosecuting its useful labors with vigorous enterprise, skill and success.

LITERARY SOCIETIES.

Among the early settlers, were some very inquiring, investigating minds. They were not disposed to receive sentiments on trust. They often met and discussed philosophical, metaphysical or moral subjects. In these interviews, much thought was elicited. All their mental powers were called into vigorous and healthful exercise. Their minds were thus expanded and strengthened. They acquired the power of reasoning with consecutive force. They, indeed, needed some one more "thoroughly instructed in the things pertaining to the kingdom of God," to throw light upon their inquiring minds. Some of them were led into important errors, and became skeptical in regard to revealed religion. They narrowly escaped making "shipwreck of the faith;" and had not God graciously interposed, by the pouring out of his Spirit, in 1799 and 1800, some of them would, doubtless, have plunged into the dark, fearful gulph of infidelity.

The Social Library which they established, contained some choice reading. Several have been successively established since, in different sections of the town. But the multiplication of periodicals has, to some extent, superseded the use of Libraries. But this, instead of having expanded and strengthened the intellect, or improved the heart, by rendering its moral principles more sound and strong, has rather induced a superficial mode of reasoning, and laxness of moral principle.

Different Societies were instituted at different periods, designed and adapted to develop and strengthen the intellect and to correct the obliquities of the heart. Among these may be mentioned the

ANDERSON INSTITUTION.

This was organized March 20, 1827. The first article of the Constitution was, "The object shall be mutual instruction in the sciences, as connected with the mechanic arts and agriculture; and the discussion of such subjects as are of a practical nature and have a bearing on the common concerns of life." Members were to pay to the Society two dollars annually, except minors, who paid one dollar. The regular meetings were held monthly; special meetings, at the discretion of the Directors. The payment of ten dollars at a time, constituted Life Membership. The officers were, a President, Secretary and Treasurer, who, with two others, were the Directors.

They were elected annually. There were thirty-nine members. The first officers were,

THOMAS J. LEE, *President*,
PLINY HARRIS, *Secretary*,
SAMUEL BENJAMIN, *Treasurer*,
ISSACHAR SNELL, } *Directors.*
JOSEPH FAIRBANKS, }

April 3, a lecture was given, on the first principles of astronomy, by Rev. John Butler. This was repeated on the 17th. May 10, there were philosophical discussions in writing, by the members. June 5, there were verbal discussions, and remarks by the President, on history and the use of terrestrial globes. August 7, Lessons were recited in Blair's Philosophy. At the next annual meeting the officers elected, were,

THOMAS J. LEE, *President*,
SAMUEL WOOD, JR., *Secretary*,
SAMUEL BENJAMIN, *Treasurer*,
DR. I. SNELL, } *Directors.*
JOSEPH FAIRBANKS, }

A public address was given by Mr. Charles Snell, and lectures on electricity by the members. They had lectures and experiments on chemistry and electricity, chemical affinity and chrystalization, and on botany, by the members and others.

1828, June 27, females were "admitted as members, free of expense, upon condition, they attend regularly to some studies, such as they may choose, which come within the objects of the Constitution." At the meeting in July, a female class recited in Blair's Philosophy.

At the annual meeting, October, 1828, the officers chosen, were,

THOMAS J. LEE, *President,*
MARK FISHER, *Secretary,*
SAMUEL BENJAMIN, *Treasurer,*
JAMES CURTIS, } *Directors.*
NATHAN FOSTER, }

Generally, during the winter, the ladies had recitations in Blair's Philosophy and Wilkins' Astronomy. Lectures were also given by members, on astronomical and philosophical subjects, illustrated by experiments.

October, 1829, the officers were,

SAMUEL WEBB, *President,*
THOMAS J. LEE, *Secretary,*
SAMUEL BENJAMIN, *Treasurer,*
DAVID THURSTON, } *Directors.*
JAMES CURTIS, }

At the meeting in November, the writer of this gave an address "on the object and advantages of the Institution." During the ensuing winter, there were lectures and discussions, by members, on mineralogy, botany, philosophy, geography, chemistry, natural history, and recitations in chemistry, astronomy, philosophy and botany.

At the next annual meeting, the same officers were re-elected. The meetings have been entertaining and profitable. But the interest in them began to decline. The meetings were neither as frequent nor as fully attended as they had been. What a tendency in human nature to degenerate! Almost invariably, attendance on the most useful, the best institutions, at length decrease s

A constant effort must be made to preserve a due regard to what might be highly beneficial. Such was the declension, that, December 26, 1831, it was "voted to dissolve the Institution."

FRANKLIN SOCIETY.

In 1832, a debating club was formed, called, "The Franklin Society." The object of this Society was, "the increase and diffusion of useful knowledge."*

LYCEUMS.

Lyceums have been repeatedly established, before which, Lectures have been publicly given on various important subjects. Citizens of the town and gentlemen from abroad have been called to the service. In the winters of 1852—3, and of 1853—4, the interest in these institutions was more general and deeper than in any preceding seasons. These lectures enlarged the sphere of knowledge, as well as afforded pleasant amusement.

Bacon said, "Knowledge is power." Hobbs said, "Wealth is power." They were both right. Both are believed. Hence, those ambitious of literary distinction, make knowledge the all absorbing object of pursuit. They are seen by the midnight lamp, "studying unto paleness." The others, incessantly plodding how they may gain the most and expend the least, are seen rising before the light, and toiling till after the stars appear. No means, which promise success in the pursuit of wealth, are left untried. Knowledge, under the control of the

* The writer has not been able to come at the records of this Society, or to learn but very little in regard to it.

gospel of Christ, is a much more desirable power than wealth. The path to knowledge now lies open to all, in our country, except the enslaved. Prior to the reformation, in the 16th century, science and literature were confined to the cloister and the university. But it has been truly said, that "more has been done in the last three centuries, by the Protestants, in the profound and comprehensive, the exact, rational, liberal development, culture and application of every valuable department of knowledge, both theoretical and practical, with a view to public and private improvement, than has been done by all the rest of the world, both ancient and modern, since the days of Lycurgus." Learning need not now be the exclusive privilege of the few professional characters. How much more rational and consistent for the young to employ time and money in educating the head and heart, than the heels. How much more in character for intelligent, accountable beings, to spend leisure hours in the well selected Library, or the well conducted Lyceum, than in the ball room, the billiard saloon, or the theater.

What men have done, men may do. Cincinnatus, while following the plow, acquired such an amount of knowledge, and such weight of character, that he was appointed Dictator of Rome. Demosthenes owed his superiority as an orator, not "to his native endowments," but to his indomitable energy and perseverance. What attainments the Tinker of Elstow made by meditation, study and prayer. Franklin was a printer's boy. By his almost unassisted efforts, he rose to a distinguished rank among the philosophers of his age. Rittenhouse was brought up in the healthful, honorable occupation of a tiller of the soil. By economising his time, he became famous as a mechanic and an astronomer. He succeeded Franklin in the Presidency of the Philosophical Society. Roger Sherman, from the bench of a cordwainer, rose to a distinguished seat in the Congress of the United States. By his assiduity and integrity, he became a renowned statesman. Think from what humble and obscure poverty, Rev. Jonas King, D. D., has become the famous Missionary at Athens in Greece. Remember Elihu Burrit, the learned blacksmith. See him mastering the Latin, Greek, Hebrew and other grammars from books fastened to the side of his shop chimney, as he blows the bellows to heat his iron. He becomes a proficient in several ancient and not a few modern languages. He is now laboring to prevail on the nations to "beat their swords into plowshares and their spears into pruning hooks; and to learn war no more." May the God of peace speed him and all his coadjutors in that truly benevolent enterprise. Let others imitate such examples.

CHAPTER IX.

Water-Cure Establishment—Marriages and deaths—Genealogical Register.

WATER-CURE ESTABLISHMENT.

Among the other means of restoring health and prolonging life in this town, the Hydropathic Establishment of Josiah Prescott, M. D., holds an important place. He has an exceedingly eligible and delightful situation, easily accessible from the surrounding country, by the Kennebec and Androscoggin Rail Road and stages. He has good accommodations for patients. In addition to his long experience as a regular practitioner, he has had eight or nine years acquaintance with the Water-Cure treatment. Under his care, many invalids are annually experiencing the restorative and invigorating efficacy of a judicious application of cold water. The virtues of this simple remedy are known only to a very limited extent. It may be doubted whether one half of them are yet understood Like other principles in the natural world, which we are just beginning to know how to apply to useful purposes, we may well believe that the preventive and healing efficacy of water, cold and warm, is yet but very imperfectly known. Experiments will, doubtless, continue to be made, until it shall be fully ascertained, that no beverage is so well adapted to perfect the human constitution in health and vigor as pure water distilling from the cloulds, or issuing from the crystal fountain. No lotion is to be compared with the various kinds of water produced by the infinite skill and benevolence of the Creator. When men will consent to use His simple preparations, unmixed with narcotics and poisons, they will be more free from diseases of both body and mind. Life will be lengthened, and will pass more peacefully and pleasantly, and will be far more useful and happy.

MARRIAGES AND DEATHS.

DEA. ENOCH WOOD kept a record of the deaths in town from 1802 to 1806, inclusive. He made the number about three times as many as were entered upon the town records. The number of deaths prior to 1802, are from the records of the town. So that it is altogether reasonable to conclude that more persons died than is stated. The writer made a record of the deaths in town from February 22, 1807, to November 21, 1851, as far as they came to his knowledge. It is not improbable there may have been a few more, but very few. It was generally known that he kept such a record, and was accustomed to mention the names of the deceased in public, on the first Sabbath in January, each year. Those who knew of deaths, of which he would not be likely to hear, were in the habit of naming them to him.

Date.	Marriages.	Deaths.	Date.	Marriages.	Deaths.
1769,	0	1	1797,	0	5
1770,	0	1	1798,	4	5
1771,	0	1	1799,	13	3
1773,	0	2	1800,	9	2
1774,	1	0	1801,	0	7
1775,	0	3	1802,	2	13
1776,	1	2	1803,	1	16
1777,	1	1	1804,	4	15
1778,	4	2	1805,	5	16
1779,	2	0	1806,	6	12
1780,	1	2	1807,	12	12
1781,	10	4	1808,	11	8
1782,	4	3	1809,	8	14
1783,	1	3	1810,	2	15
1784,	0	2	1811,	3	15
1785,	6	3	1812,	4	12
1786,	2	8	1813,	4	11
1787,	3	3	1814,	12	37*
1788,	20	1	1815,	12	14
1789,	16	2	1816,	12	15
1790,	11	4	1817,	24	8
1791,	12	3	1818,	20	13
1792,	20	8	1819,	12	21
1793,	16	1	1820,	11	14
1794,	19	4	1821,	8	17
1795,	0	2	1822,	13	32†
1796,	3	2	1823,	16	22

* This year was memorable for the prevalence of what was called "the cold, or spotted fever," in many parts of New England. Seventeen persons died of this fever between February 4 and April 23.

† Seven of these were more than seventy years of age, and one ninety-one years and eight months, and one ninety-two years. This year, ten died of cholera-morbus, and nine of dysentery. This mortality was supposed to be occasioned by the giving way of the dam at the outlet of the pond, south of the village. In con-

1824,	15	26	1840,	3	35
1825,	15	26	1841,	12	24
1826,	16	28	1842,	13	27
1827,	17	17	1843,	12	22
1828,	11	25	1844,	13	32
1829,	6	37	1845,	12	29
1830,	11	25	1846,	18	26
1831,	23	24	1847,	19	30
1832,	8	29	1848,	19	32
1833,	1	24	1849,	10	38
1834,	7	23	1850,	11	37
1835,	2	33	1851,	20	22
1836,	4	17	1852,	16	11
1837,	7	14	1853,	11	34
1838,	2	32	1854,	14	19
1839,	1	21			

Of the *thousand and thirty-seven* deaths of which the writer has an account, twenty-seven died between the ages of seventy and seventy-five, forty between the ages of seventy-five and eighty, forty between eighty and eighty-five, twenty between eighty-five and ninety, five between ninety and ninety-five, one ninety-five, one ninety-six and ten months, and one ninety-eight. Thus, in forty-four years, in a population increasing from 1,444, according to the census of 1810, to 2,154, according to the census of 1850, one hundred and thirty-five lived more than three score years and ten.

Nearly all the early settlers lived to a good old age. In a new country, abounding in hills and pure water

sequence of this, a considerable quantity of low ground, usually covered with water, was laid open to the sun. Thus was exhaled a pernicious miasma, destructive of health. All these cases occurred between July 8 and October 5; and the persons lived in the direction in which the southerly wind would waft the noxious effluvia.

gushing from perennial springs, is much which conduces to the prolonging of human life. Their food and dress are simple and plain. Their labor in the open, unpolluted air of heaven, while clearing their land and preparing it for the plough, is greatly promotive of a healthful, vigorous state of the muscular system. Their work amidst charred wood is exceedingly salubrious. For charcoal is among the most effective antiseptics. In the "hill country" of New England are formed the most robust and athletic bodies and minds.

GENEALOGICAL REGISTER.*

Benjamin Allen, married Sally Jennings. Children. Josiah, born August 6, 1788, died January 2, 1794. John Adams, born August 2, 1790, died August 19, 1790. David Larned, born August 23, 1791, died September 22, 1792. Sally, born September 14, 1793, married Cyrus Smith. Cordelia, born October 31, 1795.

Philip Allen, m Esther Tisdale. c Benjamin Mann, b January 22, 1782. Betsey, b January 3, 1785. Lemuel Craveth, b October 25, 1786. Deodate Tisdale, b October 12, 1788.

Daniel Allen, son of Edmund, b in Franklin, Massachusetts, m Sarah Delano. c Hannah, b May 4, 1783, d May 19, 1793. Cynthia, b April 10, 1784, d January, 1790. Lucinda, b December 3, 1785. Olive, b Nov.

---

* I regret not to be able to make this Register more complete, but circumstances have rendered it impracticable. The following abbreviations are used: b for born, m for married, c for children, d for died.

22, 1787. Hannah, b March 19, 1790. Luther, b March 8, 1792. Eliab, b February 18, 1794, m Hannah Jones, November 13, 1817. Sally, b January 30, 1796, Nabby, b April 4, 1798.

Oliver Allen, m Lavinia ——. c Rufus, b December 16, 1773, m Abigail Fairbanks, daughter of Benjamin Fairbanks, Sen.

William Armstrong, m Hannah ——. c William, Jr., b July 18, 1775, d April 10, 1777.

David Atkins, m Pamela Evans. c Mary, b July 11, 1787. David, b September 30, 1789. John, b January 20, 1793.

Thomas Atkinson, m Lydia Norris, January 6, 1791.

Moses Ayer, m Sarah ——. c William, b December 24, 1772.

Josiah Bacon, m Eunice Mitchell, d November 16, 1819. c Betsey, b June 15, 1793. Josiah, Jr., b March 18, 1795. Warren, b October 31, 1796. Joseph, b November 22, 1800, d February 20, 1827.

Joseph Baker, m Dorcas ——. c Elisabeth, b October 19, 1770. Mary, b November 10, 1772. Lemuel, b September 16, 1774. Joseph, Jr., b July 11, 1776.

Ebenezer Barrows, m Susanna Cushman. c Andrew, b May 30, 1777. Susanna, b October 11, 1781, m —— Harris. John, b April 21, 1784, m Deborah Perkins.

Micah Barrows, m Lucy Miller, of Middleborough, Massachusetts. c Deborah Morton, b May 24, 1799.

Peleg Benson, b in Middleborough, Massachusetts, m Sally Page, b Kensington, N. H., daughter of Simon Page. c Hannah, b August 10, 1794, m Abisha Benson.

Gustavus Adolphus, b March 10, 1796. Peleg, Jr.' b March 26, 1798, m Camilla Snell, daughter of Dr. Issachar Snell. Gustavus Adolphus, b December 9, 1799, m Hannah Page, and Miss —— Legget. Samuel Page, b November 28, 1804, m Elisabeth Mann.

Reuben Besse, m Kezia ——. c Deborah, b October 19, 1768. Reuben, Jr., b July 24, 1770. Abigail, b Jan. 17, 1773. Jonathan, b July 24, 1775, m Asenath Smith.

Samuel Besse, m Rebecca ——. c Alden, b February 21, 1795. John, b April 7, 1797. Andrew Blunt, b August 11, 1799.

William Bickford, m Polly Barden, March 6, 1800.

Jesse Bishop, son of Jesse B., m Patience Titus, daughter of John Titus, September 22, 1799.

Nathaniel Bishop, b September 17, 1766, m Judith H. Gilbert, b January 1, 1773. c Hiercy, b January 20, 1792, m Sarah Carlton. Hannah, b February 15, 1794, m Miller Shaw. Nathan, b December 13, 1796, m Martha Wing. Cyrus, b January 26, 1798, m Susan Stanley and Olive Harris. William, b November 23, 1800, m Paulina Tinkham. Ransom, b January 9, 1803, m Harriet Wood. Nathaniel Cony, b January 21, 1805, m Sarah Lane. Joseph S., b August 16, 1807, m —— Brigham. Rebecca Jane, b July 14, 1810, m Joseph Stanley. Drusilla, b April 24, 1814, m Elijah Townsend.

Squier Bishop, b in Rehoboth, Massachusetts, 1732, m Patience Titus, b 1729. c Patience, m Mathew Bragg. October 30, 1776. Mary, m Joseph Philbrick, January 3, 1782. Squier, Jr. Waitstill, m Thomas Whittier, March 22, 1781. Amy, m John Pullen.

John Blount, b in Sturbridge, Massachusetts, m Rebecca Streeter, and Margaret McCartha. c of John and Rebecca, Mary, b February 19, 1772, m William Atkinson. Rebecca, b December 17, 1773, m —— Besse. c of John and Margaret, Naomi, b December 16, 1791. John, Jr., b June 27, 1793. Martha, b March 18, 1795.

Andrew Blount, son of John, m Merideth Monk. c Jerusha, b July 17, 1789. Sophia, b March 6, 1791. Kezia, b March 31, 1793. Bethinia, b April 13, 1795. Olive, b April 17, 1797.

Beriah Bonney, m Nancy Pullen, July 1, 1798. c Lydia, b October 7, 1798, m —— Parmeter.

Isaac Bonney, m Hannah Soule. c James, b January 11, 1782, m Cynthia Cole. Hannah, b July 27, 1785, m John Jackson. Isaac, b November 1, 1787, m Hephzibah Joy.

Mrs. Hannah Bonney, m Silas Lambert. c Jarvis, b September 11, 1793, m Rebecca Holland, and Hannah Holland. Olive, b August 19, 1795, m Samuel Webb.

Benjamin Brainerd, m Ruth Delano, December 14, 1779. c Benjamin, Jr., September 1, 1780, d young. James, b April 17, 1783, m Sarah Jameson, and Deborah Brainerd. Molly, b August 21, 1784, m Samuel Richards. Sarah, b April 1, 1786, m Parsons Smith. Oren, b March 3, 1788, m Sarah Hearld.

Reuben Brainerd, m Fanny Allen, January 12, 1787. c Susanna, b February 18, 1789, m Jonas Packard, April 3, 1810. Deborah, b November 28, 1790, m James Brainerd. Fanny, b November 28, 1792, m Jonas Packard. Reuben, Jr., b February 6, 1795. Asahel, b Feb. 7, 1797.

Timothy Brainerd, m Mehitable Metcalf, December 31, 1779. c Joseph Metcalf, b November 4, 1780, d January 7, 1781. Martha, b October 27, 1782, m Samuel Walton. Nancy, b March 9, 1786, m Moses B. Gilman. Samuel, b August 3, 1796.

Nathaniel Brewster, m Betsey Pullen, daughter of Stephen Pullen, November 29, 1792. c Stephen, b March 31, 1793. Lewis, b June 3, 1795. Nancy, b September 15, 1797, m —— Dinsmore.

Jeremiah Brown, son of Unite Brown, m Mary Daily, April 24, 1793. c Hannah, b February 7, 1794, d Jan. 14, 1795. Joseph, b November 26, 1795. Abiel Daily, b March 5, 1798.

John Brown, jr., m Hannah Oldham. c Elisabeth, b September 30, 1796. Hannah, b May 21, 1798,

Joseph Brown, m Mary ——. c John, b August 29, 1774.

Unite Brown, m Rebecca Arnold. c Rebecca, m Thomas Craig. Jeremiah, m Mary Daily. John, m Mary Oldham.. Dorcas, m Alexander Thompson. Joseph, d young. Mary, m Solomon Towle. William. m Polly Cochran, March 25, 1800, and —— Gazelon. Dolly, m Reuben Ham.

Ede Hall Burgin, m Elizabeth ——. c Joseph Young, b Mar. 26, 1773.

Joseph Butterfield, m Mary ——. c Calvin, b March 31, 1797.

Lemuel Capen, m Michael ——. c Uriah, b Jan. 28, 1790. Hannah, b July 9, 1792, m Abraham Pinkham. Dorcas, b April 9, 1794. Lemuel, Jr., b Sept. 4, 1798.

David Chandler, son of John, sen. m Sally Pullen, June 9, 1796. c William Pullen, b March 9, 1800. Jacob Chandler, son of Jacob, brother of John, sen. m Deborah Chandler, March 29, 1792.

Joel Chandler, son of John, sen. b Sept. 10, 1757, m Deborah Jennings. c Noah, b Dec. 28, 1784, m —— Weeks. Joel, b June 9, 1786. Joseph, b Aug. 4, 1788, d Sept. 17, 1812. Susanna, b Sept. 21, 1790. Fayette, b Feb, 26, 1792, m —— Weeks. Deborah, b June 10, 1794, m Enoch Farnham, July 6, 1817.

John Chandler, m Lydia ——. c John, jr., b Nov. 17, 1754, m Hannah Streeter. Noah, b April 25, 1756. Joel, b Sept. 10, 1757, d April 19, 1794. Lydia, b July 5, 1759. Kezia, b April 17, 1761. Molly, b March 9, 1763, m Dr. Moses Wing, Sept. 1780. Lucy, b March 7, 1765. Susanna, b July 22, 1766, d Jan. 7, 1771. Hannah, b Jan. 19, 1768, m Daniel Marrow, jr., Sept. 20, 1786. Rhoda, b Aug. 21 1769. Susanna, b Sept. 3, 1792. David, b Jan. 6, 1775.

John Chandler, jr., b November 17, 1754, m Hannah Streeter, b March 15, 175–, June, 1783. c Alfred, b September 16, 1784, m Elioenai Stevens. John, 3d, b August 9, 1786, m Julia Harris, September 17, 1817, d June 14, 1821. Levi, b November 14, 1787, m Clarissa Foster. Milton, b March 31, 1789, m Nancy Thomas, June 22, 1817, d October 10, 1833. Tillotson, b September 12, 1790, m Tryphena Sears. Samuel, b April 16, 1792, m Deborah M. Shaw, September 10, 1823. Hannah, b October 21, 1793, m Israel Perley, November 3, 1817. Lydia. b January 31, 1795, m Dr.

Oliver Prescot, July 16, 1721. Sophia, b April 12, 1796, m Cornelius B. Morton, November 3, 1817, d Sept., 1850. Daniel, b Febrnary 1, 1798, d December, 1804. Calvin, b October 13, 1799, m —— Howard.

Samuel Chandler m Rebecca ——. c Samuel, jr., b February 18, 1777. Moses, b November 6, 1778. Jacob, b March 9, 1781.

Timothy Clement, m Lucinda Pullen, daughter of James Pullen, January 5, 1800.

Jabez Clough, b April 20, 1752, m Mary ——, b April 27, 1755. c Elisabeth, b in Hallowell, March 24, 1775. Sarah, b August 8, 1777. James, b September 3, 1779. Daniel b September 17, 1781. Noah, b May 26, 1784. Dolly, b September 20, 1786. Mary, b March 26, 1789.

Richard Colburn, m Prudence Barnes, April 14, 1796.

John Cole, m Anner ——. c Nathan, b May 3, 1786, m —— Pollard. William, b November 13, 1788. Lydia, b August 7, 1790, m Thomas Elmes. John, jr., b April 19, 1791. Cyrus, b June 13, 1792, d March 4, 1814. Hiram, b December 9, 1793, m Lois Young. Susanna, b January 31, 1796, m —— Chase. Lewis, b May 13, 1798. Morril, b December 16, 1799, m Dorothy Joy.

Samuel Cole, m Lydia ——. c John, b May 2, 1793. Eunice, b December 30, 1794. Hannah, b September 29, 1796.

John Comings, m Ruth White. c John, jr., b Jan. 5, 1781, m Mercy Barrows. Sarah, b July 3, 1785. Jason, b October 25, 1787, m Anna Miller. Amos, b October 12, 1789. David, b December 24, 1791, d January 31, 1792. Zilpha, b January 24, 1793, m Richard Stewart. Moses Cass, b January 22, 1795, m Mary Murrey. Susanna, b September 19, 1797. Ruth, b Nov. 1, 1799.

Thomas Craig, m Rachel Huntoon, January 10, 1791.

Jonathan Currier, m Phebe Lambert, daughter of Gideon Lambert, April 30, 1793. c Jonathan, jr., b Nov. 27, 1793, m Polly Sweet, December 23, 1819. Sally, b February 9, 1796, m Daniel Daily. Franklin, b Nov. 13, 1797, m Prudence Luce. Daniel Searls, b December 3, 1799.

Dr. Samuel Currier of Readfield, m Patience Stanley, daughter of Solomon Stanley, 1799.

Josiah Cushman, b in Plymouth, Massachusetts, Feb. 20, 1752, m Patience ——, b in Middleborough, Mass., July 22, 1751. c Patience, b October 21, 1774. Rufus, b January 20, 1777. John, b February 16, 1779. Sarah, b June 26, 1781, d April 27, 1782. Josiah, b June 28, 1783. Sarah, b April 18, 1787. Elias, b Dec. 20, 1789.

Jonathan Danielson of Phippsburgh, m Nancy Gilbert, daughter of Nathaniel Gilbert, 1799.

Ebenezer Davenport, b in Dorchester, Massachusetts, m Mary Crane, b in Milton, Massachusetts. c Polly, b April 10, 1768, m Abiel Walton. Rufus, b July 8, 1770. Isaac, b December 17, 1771, d October 2, 1797. Elijah, b November 15, 1773. Mercy, b July 10, 1775, m Samuel Humphrey. These were born in Dorchester, Massachusetts. Anna, b February 20, 1778, d April 24, 1783. Melatiah b January 23, 1780, m —— Lawrence. Hannah, b June 27, 1782. Ebenezer, b June 27, 1785, d January 18, 1787. Anna, b July 16, 1787, m Uriah

Holt Gray. Ebenezer, b March 10, 1791. Charlotte, b March 12, 1793.

Elijah Davenport, son of Ebenezer, 1st, m Mercy Towne. c Rufus, b November 8, 1796, m Anna Stevens. Samuel Wood, b September 30, 1798. Jonathan Belden, b December 5, 1800.

Isaac Davenport, son of Ebenezer Davenport, m Susanna Walton. c James, b June 3, 1791. Fanny, b Nov. 6, 1793. Philena, b February 9, 1796.

Barzillai Delano, b 1756, m Elisabeth Delano, daughter of Reuben. c Francis, b August 5, 1780. Sophia, b December 26, 1783. Caleb, b November 25, 1785. Betsey, b November 23, 1787. Mary, b April 10, 1790. Hannah, b May 11, 1792. Julia, b December 11, 1793. Silvia, b May 17, 1796. Barzillai, jr., b May 1, 1798. Ruth, b June 4, 1800,

Ichabod Delano, m Lucy ——. c Lydia Bartlett, b March 20, 1798. Beriah, b November 19, 1800.

James Delano, son of Zebedee, b Mar. 6, 1758, m Polly ——. c Abel, b October 5, 1785.

Seth Delano m Lydia Chandler, and Rebecca ——. c of Seth and Lydia, Rachel, b April 9, 1777. c of Seth and Rebecca, Hannah, b March 2, 1783.

Zebedee, son of John Delano, b February 27, 1727, m Sarah ——, b May 21, 1729. c Seth, b November 10, 1751, m Rebecca ——. Ruth, b April 6, 1755, m Aaron Stevens. James, b March 6, 1758. Jabez, b May 7, 1760. Sarah, b March 1, 1763. Zebedee, jr., b October 25, 1767, m Abigail Cottle, March 17, 1791. Ebenezer, b April 8, 1771, m Nancy Titus, October 24, 1793.

William Dewey, son of Rebecca, b March 25, 1793.

Constant Dexter, m Rebecca Billington. c Mary, b January 20, 1796. Lois, b February 20, 1797.

Freeman Dexter, m Polly Thurston. c Nathaniel, b in New Sandwich, August 15, 1795, m Mary Rich. Arvin, b January 15, 1797. Freeman, jr., b December 12, 1798, m Abigail Harvey. Sumner, b Oct. 26, 1800.

Thomas Eastman, m Sarah Comins, March 29, 1792. c Edward, b June 1, 1793, m —— Coleman. David, b October 20, 1794, m Selinda Wood. Polly, b Sept. 29, 1796, d April 12, 1798. Sally, b Sept. 7, 1798.

Ezekiel Eldrige, m Mary ——. c Hannah, b March 19, 1786. Ezekiel, jr., b July 31, 1788.

Solomon Esty, b May 17, 1744, O. S., m Hannah Leonard, b June 17, 1748, O. S. c Mary, b September 15, 1770, m Benjamin Reed. Nancy, b November 28, 1771, m Moses Wood, January 12, 1792. Merideth, b August 10, 1773, married Jos. Matthews. Hannah, b May 21, 1775. Lovina, b February 6, 1777, d March 26, 1777. Ebenezer, b March 27, 1778. Leonard, b September 9, 1780. Lovina, b October 27, 1782, m David Fuller. Solomon, jr., b November 20, 1784, m Dolly Fifield. Aaron and Miriam, b December 12, 1786; Aaron m Apphia Coy, and Miriam m Daniel Coy. Martha, b November 19, 1789. Betsey, b March 7, 1792, d December 22, 1812.

Abijah Fairbanks, b in Medway, Massachusetts, Jan., 1746, m Mary Clark, b February, 1750, came to Winthrop in 1800. c Olive, b September, 1759,m Joseph Metcalf. Mary, b 1773, and d young. Asa, b February 24, 1779, m Hannah Partridge.

Benjamin Fairbanks, m Keturah Luce, who was the

mother of his children. c Joseph, b July 24, 1774, m —— Eaton, d September 12, 1831. Nabby, b February 9, 1776. Benjamin, jr., b March 20, 1778, m Lydia White. Betsey, b March 20, 1780, m James Smith. Sarah, b January 6, 1782, m Joseph Norris. Lucy, b November 29, 1785, m Bartlet Allen. Deborah, b January 16, 1788, m Ichabod Foster. Dennis, b April 16, 1790, m Hannah Foster. His second wife was Sally Blue.

Elijah Fairbanks, m Elisabeth Hopkins, August 15, 1781; he d May, 1836, aged 79, and she d July 28, 1838, aged 76. c Silvia, b August 9, 1781. Elijah, jr., b December 18, 1782, m —— Allen. Polly, b Feb. 27, 1785, d May 27, 1786, Enos, b December 14, 1787, m Olive Allen. Asenath, b April 5, 1790, m John Harvey. James, b September 12, 1792. Jesse L., b Nov. 19, 1794. John, b May 26, 1797. Hannah, b March 6, 1800, m Nathan Foster.

Joseph Fairbanks, m Sybil Grover. c David, b July 17, 1777, m Lydia York. Levi, b August 12, 1778, m Hannah York, August 30, 1798. Susanna, b Sept. 8, 1779, m Gideon Lambert. Abigail, b January 2, 1781, m John Hanscom. Joanna, b July 24, 1782, m David Moody. Elias, b December 19, 1783, m Rhoda Cram. Fanny, b May 11, 1785, m Enos Jewel. Polly, b Feb. 5, 1787, m Daniel Butler. Sybil, b December 17, 1788, m Alpheus Drake. Joseph, b December 17, 1790, m Polly Richmond. Joel, b September 24, 1792, m Judith Bradford. Pamela, d December 22, 1810. Rufus, b October 16, 1794. Sally, b June 10, 1796, m Thomas Becket.

Nathaniel Fairbanks, b July 15, 1754, m Susanna Metcalf, b May 27, 1759, m October 21, 1778; she d Sept. 24, 1791. c Hannah, b Dec. 20, 1781, m Liberty Stanley. Philo, b February 21, 1784, m Susan Besse. Calvin, b August 5, 1789, m Hannah Thompson. His second wife was Lydia Chipman. c Columbus, b Nov. 7, 1793, m Lydia Wood Tinkham. Franklin, b June 18, 1795, m Hannah Cushing. Susanna, b December 15, 1796, m Rev. David Starret.

Timothy Farrington, m Sarah Pullen; he d February 1, 1799. c Preston, b August 6, 1782. Lydia, b Nov. 11, 1785, m —— Bragg. Sarah, b December 14, 1786. Hannah, b May 3, 1789. Rebecca, b May 20, 1790. Pliny, b June 3, 1792. Roxana, b Feb. 1, 1795. Jason, b September 23, 1797.

Ebenezer Fisher, m Abigail ——. c Phebe, b Sept. 6, 1784. Reuben, b March 1, 1786. Jesse, b April 7, 1788.

Daniel Foster, son of Timothy, jr., m Betsey Cole, January 17, 1799. c Olive, b March 3, 1800.

David Foster, son of Timothy, sen., m Melicent How, daughter of Ichabod How, January 13, 1783. c Anna, b December 11, 1783, m Thomas Stevens. Ichabod, b June 9, 1785, m Deborah Fairbanks. Preston, b April 30, 1788. Clarissa, b August 6, 1790. Lavinia, b July 8, 1792, d November 5, 1792. Freeman, b December 30, 1793, m Lydia White, d September 14, 1847. David, jr., b July 4, 1795, m Harmony, daughter of Joseph Packard. Nathan, b March 2, 1798, m Hannah, daughter of Elijah Fairbanks. John Winthrop, b Feb. 12, 1800.

Otis Foster, son of Timothy, jr., m Lucy Norris. c Phebe, b September 18, 1800.

Richard Foster, son of Timothy, sen., m Clarissa Barton, October 21, 1791. c Parthenia, b May 18, 1792. Ebenezer, b August 14, 1794. Harlow Barton, b Sept. 12, 1798.

Steuart Foster, b April 8, 1757, m Jerusha Wadsworth. c Wadsworth, b January 7, 1788, m Lucinda Snell, Abigail Kezer and L. Hayward. Oliver, b Aug. 29, 1789, m Lydia Perkins, November 30, 1815. Sibyl, b July 21, 1791, m Benjamin Robbins, June 22, 1817. Moses, b November 10, 1793, m Temperance Davis. Eunice, b January 4, 1796, m Isaac Shaw, jr. Isaac, b April 22, 1798, m Lois Hoyt, January 25, 1821. Steuart, jr., b June 7, 1800, m Mary Ames.

Samuel Foster, b June 26, 174–, m September 22, 1764, Leah Avery, b in Rumbouts, N. Y., May 22, 1749. c Ebenezer, b in Rumbouts, Sept. 26, 1766. Richard, b at Little nine Partners, May 31, 1768. Mary, b at Little nine Partners, August, 1770, m Edward Washburne. Desire, b November 5, 1772, at Rhinebec, N. Y., m Abraham Fuller of Livermore, 1799. Mercy, b at Wrentham, Mass., November 7, 1775, m Timothy Sweet, January 8, 1800. John Wilde, b at Cumberland, R. I., December 29, 1778. Eliphalet, b in Winthrop, October 20, 1780. William, b October 6, 1782. Benjamin, b June 17,1784. Michael, b April 5, 1786.

Capt. Timothy Foster, b May, 14, 1720, m Sibler Freeman, b October 29, 1723; he d April 3, 1785, and she d December 8, 1813. c Timothy, jr., b March 21,

1745, m Abigail Allen, d August 1, 1825. Billy, b September 24, 1747. Eliphalet, b July 27, 1749. Susan, b April 15, 1751, m Micajah Dudley. David, b May 26, 1753, m Melicent Howe, b April 25, 1762, d January 3, 1820. Thomas, b May 23, 1755. Steuart, b April 8, 1757, m Jerusha Wadsworth. John, b April 20, 1759. Oliver, b March 5, 1761. Sibler, b April 27, 1763, m Ephraim Stevens. Stephen, the first white male child born in Winthrop, b Feb. 28, 1766, m Sally Streeter.

Timothy Foster, jr., b March 21, 1745, m Abigail ——. c Otis, b May 8, 1773. Daniel, b June 3, 1775. Elisabeth, b August 29, 1777, m Isaac Perkins. Molley, b February 24, 1783. Hannah, b November 17, 1786.

John French, m Elisabeth Porter, November 4, 1790. c Nehemiah, b September 2, 1785.

Moses Frost, m Abigail French. c Betsey, b June 18, 1795. Josiah, b May 23, 1797. Moses, jr., b Dec. 11, 1798. Lydia, b December 11, 1800.

Samuel Frost, m Anna ——. c Aaron, b December 14, 1767. Moses, b March 3, 1770. Lydia, b Feb. 12, 1772. Noah, b June 21, 1774. William, b May 1, 1777. John, b August 3, 1779.

John Fuller, b on Cape Cod, m Anna, b in Boston. c Isaac, b Aug. 5, 1759, m Nancy Whitaker. Abraham, b Dec. 19, 1771, m Desire Foster, daughter of Samuel F., 1799. Nathan, b Oct. 21, 1774. Anna, b Sept. 16, 1777, d Nov. 6, 1797. John, jr., b Feb. 13, 1779. Lydia, b July 20, 1782. Desire, b Apr. 2, 1785, m Henry Caslin. Thomas, b Sept. 26, 1787. Addison, b Dec. 27, 1790. Nabby, b Dec. 13, 1793, m Henry Hawkins, a Methodist preacher.

Francis Fuller, m Hannah ——. c Hannah, b Aug. 19, 1773. Mary, b May 1, 1775.

Peter Gale, m Jerusha Rice. c Orpheus Burgin, b Jan. 16, 1799. Eliza, b Apr. 21, 1800.

Nathaniel Gilbert, m Hannah Hemps. c Rebecca, b March 3, 1774, m Zachariah Butterfield.

James Goud, m Joanna ——. c Margaret, b July 29, 1772. Rachael, b June 11, 1788. James, jr., b June 13, 1790. Ezekiel, b Oct. 26, 1792. William, son of James and Nancy G., b June 29, 1795. Charlotte, b April 30, 1797. Nancy, b Feb. 14, 1799.

Lazarus Goud, m Lurania ——. c Betsey, b March 28, 1786. Rachel, b Dec. 18, 1789. George, b Jan. 28, 1791. Rahannas, b Jan. 27, 1793.

Clarkson Goud, son of Patty G., b March 27, 1788.

John Gray, m Sarah ——. William, b Jan. 30, 1774, in Hallowell. Frederic, b June 29, 1775, in Hallowell. Sarah, b June 13, 1787, in Hallowell. John, jr., b June 13, 1779, in Winthrop.

Seth Greely, m Jane ——. c Moses, b Nov. 27, 1777, in Hallowell.

Josiah Hall, m Amiable ——. c Nathan, b Jan. 22, 1765. Allen, b Jan. 29, 1767. Abigail, b April 13, 1769. Mary, b Aug. 27, 1771, d May 23, 1795. Esther, b Jan. 4, 1774.

Nathan Hall, m Elizabeth ——; he died Oct. 26, 1775. c Mary, b March 12, 1773. Abijah, b Oct. 21, 1774. Betsey, b Feb. 26, 1776, m John Shed.

Preserved Hall, m Abigail ——. c Josiah, b May 16, O. S., 1743.

Charles Harris, son of Obadiah, b in Wrenthan, Mass, m Meletiah Hawes. c Timothy, b Oct. 9, 1784. Harmon, b July 22, 1786. Julia, b Sept. 10, 1788, m John Chandler and John May. Caleb, b June 15, 1790, m Dorcas Cole. Pliny, b Feb. 20, 1792, m Lucy Foster. Cynthia, b Feb. 21, 1794, m Jacob Cochran. Obadiah, b Nov. 18, 1795. Mary, b Jan. 19, 1798, m —— Johnson. Charles, b Jan. 17, 1800.

John Harvey, m Ruth ——. c Sally, b Dec. 27, 1796.

Jonathan Hilliard m Deborah Chandler.

David Hinckley, m Huldah Read, Sept. 9, 1789. c Reuel, b Nov. 18, 1790. Hannah, b March 4, 1793. Alanson, b March 20, 1795. David, jr., b April 21, 1797. Cynthia, b March 18, 1799.

Josiah Hodges, m Tabitha ——. c Benjamin, b Oct. 7, 1797.

Frederic Howard, m Elizabeth ——. c Daniel, b July 22, 1794. Sarah, b Jan. 30, 1796. Nabby, b Aug. 4, 1797. Elizabeth, b March 11, 1799.

Ichabod Howe, m Sarah ——. c Jonathan, b July 31, 1760. Melicent, b April 25, 1762, m David Foster. Sarah, b March 15, 1766. Stephen, b Dec. 9, 1768, m Eleanor Turner. David, b Sept. 1, 1771, m Freelove Maxim. Susanna, b April 13, 1774, m Joseph York. Eunice, b Feb. 22, 1776, m Henry Wood, jr., Oct. 1, 1800.

Dr. John Hubbard, b Sept. 28, 1759, m Olive Wilson, b Jan. 23, 1762. c Olive, b March 1, 1786. Sophia, b Feb. 21, 1788. Polly, b April 26, 1790,

Richard Humphrey, m Elizabeth ——. c William, b

Oct. 6, 1777. Samuel, b Aug. 4, 1780, m MercyDavenport.

Thomas Jacobs, b in England, m Nancy——. c Mehitable, b Oct. 9, 1798, in Amesbury, Mass. Robert, b May 8, 1799, do. Elijah, b March 28, 1800, in Winthrop.

John Jewett. m Sarah ——. c John, jr., b April 2. 1779.

Moses Joy, m Huldah Soule, Oct. 1788. c Hartford, b Dec. 15, 1789, d Nov. 9, 1811. Huldah, b March 10, 1792, m Hebron Luce. Mary, b June 5, 1794, m Daniel Carr.

Jacob Judkins, m Anna Blunt. c Clarissa, b April 11, 1788. Lorrain, b Feb. 4, 1790. Rebecca ,b Feb. 16, 1792. Hannah and John Blount, b June, 4, 1794.

John Kezer, m Apphia Lancaster. c Mehitable, b Ap. 21, 1786, m Isaac French. Apphia b Aug. 26, 1789, m Nathaniel Whiting. Abigall, b Ap. 4, 1791, m Wadsworth Foster. John, jr., b Jan. 28, 1795, m Hannah, daughter of Samuel Waugh.

Ebenezer King, m Mehitable Robbins. c Amos D. b Oct. 18, 1790. Jason, b July 10, 1792. Clarissa, b July 15, 1794. Barnard, b May 10, 1796, m Jerusha Rice. Darius, b Feb. 4, 1798. Zenas, b May 10, 1800.

Samuel King, m Susanna Brainard. c Samuel, jr., b Dec. 7, 1789, m Matilda Rice. Benjamin, b March 24, 1791, m Olive Rice. Isaac. b July 2, 1792, m Martha Esty. Amasa, b March 7, 1795, m Mehitable Jacobs. Sarah, b Jan. 18, 1797, d April 15. 1814. Susanna, b Sept. 28, 1798, m Arnold Sweet. Polly, b Aug. 9, 1800, m BenjaminC. Joy.

Gideon Lambert, b in Tisbury, Martha's Vineyard, came to Winthrop 1770, m Susanna ——. c Ebenezer, b May 8, 1761. Paul, b July 16, 1763. Silas, b Oct. 15, 1765, m Hannah Soule Bonney. Beulah, b Jan. 1, 1768, The above were b in Tisbury. Susanna, b Sept. 24, 1770, m Samuel Pease. Phebe, b May 20, 1774. Gideon, jr., b June, 11, 1777, m Susanna Fairbanks.

Paul Lambert, son of Gideon and Susanna Lambert' b July 16, 1763, m Mercy Dexter, Nov. 25, 1790. c Dennis, b Oct. 7, 1791. Ebenezer, b April 6, 1793. Samuel, b Feb. 3, 1795. Polly, b Jan. 28, 1797. Paul, jr., b March 7, 1790.

Silas Lambert, son of Gideon L., m Hannah Soule Bonney. c Jarvis, b Sept. 11, 1793, m 2 sisters,(Holland.) Olive, b Aug. 19, 1795, m Samuel Webb. Silas, b May 7, 1798, d Sept. 8, 1818.

James Lane, m Eunice ——. c Anna, b May 3, 1782. Abraham Chase, b July 19, 1784. Serena, b Dec. 6, 1786. James, jr., b May 2, 1789.

Joseph Lawrence, m Joanna ——. c Abigail, b June 10, 1794. Noah, b June 3, 1796. Sally, b May 9, 1798. Francis, b Dec. 19, 1799.

Nathaniel Lovering, m Jerusha Follett. c Nathaniel, jr., b Feb. 23, 1793. Jerusha, b Oct. 31, 1895, m Albert Hayward. John, b Jan. 4, 1799, m Bathsheba Wood.

Daniel Marrow, b in Medway, Mass., m Elizabeth Harding. c Reuben, b May 14, 1780.

Daniel Marrow, jr., m Hannah Chandler. c Luther, b Aug. 20, 1787. Hannah, b Aug. 28, 1788, m James Wheeler. Achsah, b March 17, 1790, m Peasley Hoyt.

Lewis, b Nov. 19, 1791, d Dec. 25, 1791. Alice, b March 14, 1793. Daniel, 3d, b Nov. 28, 1794. Lois, b June 19, 1796. David, b June 12, 1798. Rhoda, b March 20, 1800, m Ebenezer Keen.

Ebenezer Marrow, son of Daniel M., m Abigail Fisher, Jan. 5, 1792. c Milton, b Oct. 25, 1792, m —— Lambert. Clarissa, b April 8, 1795, m —— Longfellow. Zelotes Augustus, b July 27. 1797. John Broadhead, b Oct. 22, 1799, m Lydia L. Lambert.

Samuel Marrow, m Chloe Titus. c Pamela, b Aug. 27, 1798. Lewis, b Sept. 17, 1800.

Nathaniel Marston m Elaenor Nelson. c Polly, b Nov. 19, 1799.

Joseph Matthews, m Merideth Esty. c Joseph, jr., b Dec. 29, 1796.

Joseph Metcalf, b March 30,1765, in Franklin, Mass., m Olive Fairbanks, b Sept. 5, 1759, in Wrentham, Mass., m June 17, 1790. c Isaac Newton, b April 24, 1791, d Oct. 23, 1804. Susan, b Aug. 2, 1792, d Jan. 21, 1823, Almira, b Feb. 28, 1794, m Cephas Thomas. Joseph Addison, b Dec. 25, 1795, m Chloe F. Adams, he died June 17, 1845. Olive, b Jan. 2, 1798, m Samuel Wyman. Moses Haven, b Nov. 22, 1799, m Elizabeth D. Hamilton and Eliza Baker.

Josiah Mitchell, m Eunice ——. c Betsy, b Nov. 25, 1774. Lydia, b April 25, 1777. Molly, b Dec. 3, 1780. John, b June 15, 1783.

Ebenezer Moore, m Eunice Norton, of Kittery. c Oliver, b Feb. 16, 1796. Infant, b Jan. 22, 1798, d next day. Polly Crocker, b Jan. 22, 1798, d Jan. 30, 1798. Joanna, b Dec. 25, 1798.

Ebenezer Morton, b in Middleborough, Mass., m Martha Wood and Nancy Adams. c Samuel, b July 24, 1782. son of Martha. John, b Dec. 16, 1794, d July 24, 1811. Ebenezer, Jr., b Dec. 6, 1797, sons of Nancy.

Livy Morton, b in Middleboro', Mass., m Hannah Daily, March 13, 1788. c Daniel Oliver, b Dec. 21, 1788, graduated at Middlebury College, Vt., ordained pastor of Congregational Church, Shoreham, Vt. Joseph Warren, b Aug. 25, 1793. Lendall, b March 22, 1796. The family returned to Middleborough in 1798.

Nathaniel Morton, m Christina Ling. c Silvanus. b Sept. 2, 1791. Cornelius Bennett, b Jan. 14, 1793, m Sophia Chandler, daughter of John C., jr. Theodate Bennett, b April 5, 1798. Polly, b Nov. 19, 1799.

Andrew Nelson, m Anna —. c James, b Sept 11, 1786.

Elias Nelson, m Deborah Barrows. c Sarah, b 1794. Deborah, b May 31, 1798, m Leonard Norcross. Lot Packard, b June 18, 1800. They removed to Monmouth, and Mr. Nelson became pastor of the Baptist church in Jay.

Joseph Norris, m Sally Fairbanks, daughter of Benjamin F., Nov. 24, 1785. c Velina, b Feb. 26, 1800.

Amos Perley, b in Boxford, Mass., m Sally Smith. c Frederic. Israel. Sally. Fanny. Olive, b April 28, 1793, d Sept. 1850

Benjamin Porter, m Molly Barton, d Jan. 10, 1786. c Betsey, b Sept. 13, 1779. John, b Dec. 25, 1780. Benjamin, Jr., b July 17, 1782, m Pamela Barton. Polly, b May 10, 1788.

James Prescott, son of Jedediah, Senior, b Feb. 23, 1767, m Polley Owen, b Dec. 20, 1767. c An infant d June 3, 1790. John, b March 17, 1791. Susan, b July

9, 1792. Lewis, b Aug. 17, 1793. Sally, b Jan. 25, 1795. William, b July 17, 1796. Amasa, b Nov. 1, 1797.

Jedediah Prescott, jr., b in Deerfield, N. H., Sept. 22, 1746, m Sarah Morrill, b in Salisbury, Mass., March 28, 1752. c Noah, b Dec. 1, 1773, m Betsey French. Mary, b Feb. 19, 1776, m Daniel Matthews. Ruth, b Jan. 10, 1778, m Caleb Brown. Sally, b Sept. 27, 1779. John, b Dec. 7, 1781, m Anna Drake. Betsey, b Sept. 30, 1783, d aged 4 years; these were born in Deerfield. Josiah, b Sept. 2, 1782, M. D., m Mary French. Lois, b April 25, 1788. Levi, b March 22, 1790. James Bowdoin, b March 19, 1792. Betsey, b March 31, 1794. Jedediah, 3d, b May 2, 1797. Hannah, b Sept. 8, 1800. c of Jedediah 1st—Jesse, Jedediah, jr., Samuel, James, Elijah.

Odlin Prescott, son of Benjamin, m Elizabeth ——. c Elizabeth, b Aug. 12, 1773, m Ichabod Wing. Ruth Stevens, b June 5, 1781, m Christopher Ripley. Benjamin Rowe, b Feb. 22, 1785, m Betsey Emery.

Samuel Prescott, son of Jedediah, senior, m Betty Whittier. c Benjamin, b April 24, 1782. Samuel, jr., b Sept. 4, 1783. Betty, b April 9, 1785, m —— Baker. Mary, b Dec. 11, 1788. Anna, b Nov. 18, 1790.

Jesse Prescott, son of Jedediah, senior, m Polly Whittier. c Hannah, b April 13, 1785.

John Pullen, m Amy, daughter of Squier and Patience Bishop, June 24, 1785. c Abigail, b March 31, 1786. Parthena, b April 20, 1788, m —— McPherson. Phebe, b Aug. 11, 1790. Lydia, b March 9, 1793. Olive, b Sept. 28, 1795, m —— McPherson. Cynthia, b Nov. 26, 1797, d Nov. 28, 1797. John. James. Sally B. b Dec. 15, 1798.

Jonathan Pullen, son of Stephen P., b Feb. 9, 1771, m Silva Bonney, March 5, 1794. c Cyrus, b Sept. 19, 1794. Lois, b July 11, 1796, m ——— Hinckley. Sullivan, b March 30, 1798.

Jonathan Pullen, son of James P., m Lucy Barrows, Aug. 5, 1800.

Oliver Pullen, m Abigail ——. c Sargent, b Jan. 9, 1784.

Stephen Pullen, m Mercy Blackington, d Sept. 14, 1815, aged 72. c Abigail, b Aug. 30, 1769, d Feb. 22, 1770. Jonathan, b Feb. 9, 1771, m Silva Bonney. Stephen, jr., b Jan. 12, 1773, d Feb. 25, 1773. Betsey, b Dec. 7, 1773, m Nathaniel Brewster. Stephen, jr., b Nov. 6, 1775. Mary, b Jan. 25, 1777, m Amos Stevens, jr. George b Feb. 5, 1779, m Harriet Gilbert. Nancy, b July 20, 1781, m —— Harvey. Lydia, b May 1, 1783, m Caleb Parmenter. James, b Jan. 22, 1786, m Sally Harvey. Elioenai, b April 21, 1788, m —— Harvey. Lois, b April 21, 1788. Greenleaf, b July 10, 1790, m Mary Hanscom.

George Pullen, son of Stephen P., m Harriet Gilbert, Oct. 11, 1798. c George Washington, b Dec. 31, 1798. John Adams, b Dec. 31, 1798.

William Pullen and Patience Bishop. c William, jr., b Jan. 21, 1774. William Pullen, senior, m Sarah Fairbanks. c Sally, b July 2, 1779, m David Chandler. Leonard, b July 18, 1781. James, b July 31, 1783, d Oct. 17, 1784. Clarissa, b May 11, 1786, m Dexter Pullen. Philena, b Oct. 21, 1789.

Benjamin Read, m Mary Easty. c Leonard, b Oct. 13, 1791. Polly, b March 12, 1793. Perrin and Perinthy, b June 17, 1796. Martha, b Aug. 16, 1798. Joseph, b July 9, 1800.

Joseph Rice, m Olive Allen, June 12, 1787. c Joseph. Isabel, m Isaac Nelson. Matilda, m Samuel King, jr. Olive, m Benjamin King. Jerusha, b Nov. 9, 1797, m Bernard King. Betsey, b Feb. 17, 1800.

Joseph Richards, m Sarah ——. c Samuel, b Nov. 3, 1783.

William Richards, m Joanna Whiting, daughter of Jona. W., May 6, 1785. c Anna, b April 27, 1786. Susanna, b April 7, 1788, m Benja. Packard. John, b Oct. 28, 1789, m Mary Craig. William, jr., b Nov. 13, 1791. Pliny, b Sept. 25, 1793, d Sept. 24, 1797. Elioenai. b Jan. 31, 1796. Joanna, b Jan. 6, 1799, m Rev. Josiah Houghton.

Nathan Richmond, b Middleboro, Mass., m Mary Streeter. c Abigail, b Jan. 24, 1787, m Joseph Dow, Leonard, b Jan. 25, 1789, m Nancy Sweet. Warren, b Sept. 27, 1790, m —— Jones. Mary, b May 7, 1792, m Joseph Fairbanks. Reliance, b Jan. 30, 1794, m Joseph Additon. Huldah, b June, 16, 1796, m Alson Lothrop, Nathan, jr., b Feb. 14, 1799, m Rhoda Lothrop. Salmon, b same date, m Silva Merrill.

Asa Robbins, b May 5, 1759, m Olive Clark, b July 13, 1762. c Benjamin, b Aug. 2, 1789, m Sybil Foster. Asa, jr., b July 28, 1791, m Hannah Shaw. Oliver, b April 11, 1793, m Asenath Wing. Cyrus. b Nov. 29, 1796, m Orpah Packard. Olive, b Aug. 21. 1800, m William Huse.

Daniel Robbins, b in Walpole, Massachusetts, August, 1722, m Mary Kingsbury, b August, 1732. c Mary, b

1752, m —— Fisher. Hannah, b 1754, m Peter Lyon. Daniel, jr., b February 27, 1757, m Mary Clark, and Eunice Wadsworth. Asa, b May 5, 1759, m Olive Clark, came to Winthrop, 1781. Azubah, b April 7, 1761, m David Morse. Abigail, m —— Fisher. Eleazar, b July 16, 1762, m Mehitable Ladd. Kezia, b Mar. 29, 1766, m David Manter. Mehitable, b November 7, 1797, m Ebenezer King. Deborah.

Daniel Robbins, jr., m Mary Clark. c Aquilla, b Nov. 2, 1784. Clark, b April 9, 1786. His second wife was Eunice Wadsworth. c Jerusha, b July 18, 1792, m Robert Goddard, d October 14, 1844. Hannah, b February 6, 1795, m Ezekiel Bailey, d July 28, 1828. Mary, b November 7, 1797, m Ezekiel Bailey.

Eleazar Robbins, son of Daniel, sen., b July 16, 1761, m Mehitable Ladd. c Mary, b October 14, 1797. Betsey, b April 30, 1799.

Benjamin Sanborn, m Lucy French, 1799.

Paul Sears, m Mercy Stevens, daughter of Jos. S., 1st, January 27, 1778. c John, b September 3, 1778. Moses, b December 3. 1779. Paul, jr., and Mercy, b July 5, 1781; Paul, jr., m Susan Billington, and Mercy m —— White. Silas, b March 17, 1783. Alice, b October 22, 1785, m Nathaniel Whittier. Thomas, b February 15, 1788, d October 4, 1790. Charlotte, b November 27, 1791, d September 13, 1814. Tryphena, b October 21, 1793, m Tillotson Chandler, son of John, jr.

Abraham Shaw, m Hannah Miller. c Samuel, b Feb. 18, 1785, m Martha Briggs. Sally, b October 5, 1786, m Edward Starr. Abraham, jr., b December 6, 1789.

Abishai Miller, b January 17, 1791, m Hannah Bishop, daughter of Nathaniel B. Oren, b March 26, 1793, m Eunice, daughter of Adin Stanley. Ebenezer, b July 10, 1795, m Fanny Belcher. Hannah, b July 26, 1797, m Asa Robbins, jr. Susanna, b July 15, 1799. John, b October 28, 1800.

Isaac Shaw, b in Middleborough, Mass., m Deborah Wood, daughter of Moses W., Jan. 15, 1790. c Lydia, b March 2, 1791. Isaac, jr., b October 17, 1792, m Eunice Foster, daughter of Steuart F. Earl, b December 1, 1794, m Caroline and Prescilla Thomas, daughters of Silvanus Thomas. Samuel Wood and Phebe Wood, b April 15, 1798; hed August 6, 1725.

Elisha Smith, m Susanna ——. c Beulah, b September 19, 1769. Abigail, b December 8, 1771. Susanna, b July 17, 1775. Hannah, b September 13, 1777.

Jacob Smith, m Rebecca Hopkins. c Dorothy, b April 21, 1788. Jane, b October 28, 1790. Greenleaf, b August 29, 1792. Lydia, b June 27, 1797.

Matthias Smith, m Comfort ——. c Charles, b Aug. 28, 1777. Matthias, jr., m Temperance Blossom, Nov. 24, 1785.

Ransford Smith, m Mary ——. c Abijah, b January 3, 1771. Mary, b February 24, 1776.

Adin Stanley, son of Jacob Stanley, m Silence Packard. c Lemuel, b October 29, 1784, m Mehitable Gilman, and Lucy Benjamin. Dexter, b July 8, 1787, died Sept. 3, 1807. Morrell, b January 15, 1791, m Polly Andrews, and Charlotte Gilman. Eunice, b November 9, 1793, m Oren Shaw; he d April 7, 1844.

Henry Stanley, son of Jacob Stanley, m Joanna Smith c Sewall, b September 29, 1799, m Lucy Philbrook, daughter of Charles P.

Nathaniel Stanley, m Abigail Hall. c Nathaniel, jr., b July 4, 1772. Patty, b November 21, 1775, d August 19, 1787. Nathan, b April 13, 1777. They removed early to Belfast.

Peter Stanley, son of Solomon S., m Criscinda Rice. c George Washington, b March 1800.

Rial Stanley, b March 11, 1759, m Abigail Fairbanks, b Jan. 20, 176-. c Martha, b September 5, 1783, m Nathan F. Cobb. Fanny, b October 3, 1785, m Barney Haskell. Waterman, b March 10, 1788, m Polly Richardson. Abigail, b May 16, 1791, m Fred. Lecrois. Jonathan Lee, b November 6, 1794.

Solomon Stanley, m Patience Perry. c Patience, m Dr. Samuel Currier. Liberty, b 1776. Solomon, jr., b September 15, 1780, m —— Hayward. Abigail, b March 19, 1782. Peter.

James Stanley, m Grace Tupper, April 3, 1793.

Amos Stevens, son of Joseph, b July 16, 1749, m Mary Whiting, daughter of Jonathan W., sen. c Amos, jr., b April 30, 1775. John Whiting, b October 10, 1777, d October 11, 1778. James, b January 17, 1779. Asa, b May 2, 1780, d March 26, 1783. John, b March 18, 1783. Whiting, b May 25, 1784. Levi, b April 3, 1787. Philena, b September 12, 1788, m —— Butler.

Amos Stevens, jr., m Polly Pullen. c Susanna, b March 18, 1796. Sumner, b February 10, 1797. Betsey, b June 23, 1798. Polly, b December 17, 1799.

Daniel Stevens, b January 23, 1763, m Rachel Hilliard,

b May 15, 1770. c Hannah, b March 8, 1789. Rachel, b March 26. 1791. Benjamin Hilliard, b June 10, 1793. Elisabeth, b April 12, 1795. Daniel, jr., b May 17, 1797. Sally, b October 18, 1799.

Ephraim Stevens, son of Joseph, sen., b June 29, 1758, m Sybil Foster. c Hannah, b January 6, 1783. Thomas, b May 29, 1784, m Anna Foster. Aaron, b February 26, 1786, m Ruth Delano. Ephraim, jr., b March 17, 1788. Eliphalet, b April 11, 1790. Sybil, b March 15, 1792. Joshua, b March 21, 1794. Anna, b January 20, 1796.

James Stevens, son of Amos S., m Abigail Stanley, daughter of Solomon S. c James, jr., b Nov. 5, 1800.

Joseph Stevens, b in Billerica, Massachusetts, October 20, 1720, m Elisabeth Emery, b in the same place, in 1723; he d October, 1791, and she d February 28, 1798. c Elisabeth, b October 10, 1744. Joseph, jr., b April 8, 1746, d 1747. Joseph, jr., b October 31, 1747. Amos, b July 16, 1749, m Mary Whiting, daughter of Jonathan W., February 14, 1774. Samuel, b April 28, 1751. Mercy, b November 23, 1752, m Paul Sears. Abel, b April 27, 1755. Esther, b October 6, 1756, m James Work. Ephraim, b June 29, 1758, m Sybil Foster. William, b July 4, 1760, m Susan Whiting, daughter of Jonathan W. Jonas, b April 20, 1763, m Sarah Wyman. c of Jonas and Sarah W. Stevens, Jonas, jr., b May 27, 1786, m Sarah Sprague. Sarah, b January 27, 1788. Zachariah, b June 12, 1790, and d young. Nancy, b July 1, 1792, d young. Jonas, sen., also m Elisabeth Marrow. c Timothy, b August 29, 1704, m Catharine S. Potter, in N. Y. city. He sailed from N. Y., master of a ship, and was never heard of. Philemon, b August 8, 1796, m Fidelia Smith. Benjamin, b January 5, 1799, m Camilla Howard.

Joseph Stevens, jr., m Rachel ——. c Lucy, b Feb. 17, 1774. Betty, b March 3, 1776. Joseph, 3d, b Feb. 16, 1778. Abel, b February 20, 1780. Rachel, b April 7, 1782.

Samuel Stevens, m Lois Allen. c Lois, b January 15, 1775, m —— Kendall. Samuel, jr., b March 11, 1777. Eunice, b Jan. 19, 1779. William, b Sept. 23, 1780.

William Stevens, b July 4, 1760, m Susanna Whiting, daughter of Jonathan Whiting, Esq. c Asenath, b July 11, 1784. Susanna, b October 19, 1785. Martha, b May 31, 1787. Elioenai, b February 17, 1789. Jane, b December 20, 1790. John, b September 22, 1793. Joanna, b March 31, 1795. William, jr., b July 28, 1797. Bathsheba, b November 2, 1799.

John Streeter, m Mercy ——. c Nancy, b September 13, 1786. John, jr., b December 18, 1788. Rhoda, b August 15, 1791. Clarissa, b September 27, 1793. Melinda, b April 2, 1796.

Arnold Sweet, m Polly Bonney, March 9, 1789, d March 25, 1798. c Nancy, b May 2, 1791, m Leonard Richmond, son of Nathan R. Arnold, jr., b March 21, 1793, m Susan B. King, Aug. 2, 1818. Polly, b. Aug. 30, 1796, m Jona. Currier, jr. Florena, b Feb. 10, 1798. m Samuel Wood, jr.

Ellis Sweet, m Polly Fuller. c Loren, b Aug. 7, 1796.

Jesse Sweet, m Deborah Bonney. c John, b July 23, 1800.

Alexander Thompson, m Dorcas Brown, Feb. 22, 1789. c Zilpha, b Dec. 20, 1790. Rebecca, b Jan. 26, 1793. James, b Jan. 1, 1794. Ira, b Dec. 30, 1796. Aaron, b Feb. 12, 1799.

Benjamin Tibbets, m Betsey ——. c Joseph, b Jan. 10, 1800.

John Turner, m Rachel ——. c Nancy, b Jan. 18, 1753. Sarah, b June 5, 1785. John, jr., b Nov. 24, 1788. Thomas, b June 24, 1791. James, b Feb. 1, 1794. Catharine, b July 13, 1796.

Aaron Wadsworth, m Lucy Stevens. c Aaron, jr., b Feb. 11, 1796. James, b July 26, 1797. Susanna, b May 2, 1799.

Edward Washburn, m Polly Foster, daughter of Samuel F. c Hannah, b May 3, 1791. Polly, b March 31, 1793. Cynthia, b Dec. 23, 1794. Olive, b Jan. 19, 1797. Abner Waterman, b Oct. 19, 1798. Asenath, b July 3, 1800.

John Wadsworth, m Hannah Crane. c John, jr.. b Feb. 5, 1789, m Abigail Smith. Mary, b March 5, 1791. David, d Feb. 18, 1799. Hannah, b March 16, 1792, d April 13, 1792. Isaac, b June 10, 1793, m Rebecca Hewins. Stratton, b Sept. 30, 1795, d Nov. 21, 1814. Alva, b Aug. 18, 1797. Sally, b Dec. 7, 1800.

Moses Wadsworth, m Hannah ——. c Daniel, b May 15, 1799.

Samuel Wadsworth, m Abigail ——. c Abigail, b June 23, 1791. Hannah, b June 10, 1793. Samuel, jr., b May 31, 1795. Olive, b Sept. 6, 1797.

Robert Waugh, m Elizabeth ——. c Robert, jr., b March 25, 1767, m Sally Smith, March 22, 1791. John, b Aug. 14, 1770. Samuel, b July 27, 1772, m Betsey Page, 1799. Elizabeth, b May 10, 1774. George, b Jan. 12, 1777, m Nancy Turner.

Benjamin White, m Mary ——. c Polly, b Sept. 14, 1785. Ebenezer, b Oct. 14, 1786.

Joel White, b Jan. 16, 1764, in Dedham, Mass, m Mella ——. c Moses, b Jan. 29, 1788, m Mary Low, daughter of Rev. Robert Low. Joel, jr., b July 24, 1790, m Sarah Keen. Lewis, b Dec. 17, 1792. Mella, b Feb. 5, 1795, m Jonathan Whiting, 3d. Eliza b May 6, 1797. Sarah, b March 16, 1799.

John White, m Jennette ——. c Benjamin, b May 13, 1790. Milley, b April 7, 1792. John Randall, b Jan. 1, 1792. Ambrose, b April 19, 1796. Sewall, b April 15, 1798. Thomas, b Aug. 3, 1800, d Aug. 22, 1800.

Jonathan Whiting, m Elioenai, daughter of Rev. David Thurston, Wrentham, Mass. c Elias, d May 3, 1775. John, d Dec. 10, 1775. Thurston, Mary, Susan, Joanna.

Jonathan Whitiug, jr., m Sarah Whittier, Sept. 16, 1778, and Betsey Davies. c Sarah, b Aug. 24, 1779, m Richard Kidder. Betsey, b June 9, 1781. Elioenai, b May 29, 1783, m Edmund Frost. Hannah, b Jan. 17, 1785, m Abijah Joy. Jonathan, 3d, b Nov. 7, 1786, m Susan Hathorn, Amelia White, and —— Richards. Nathaniel, b Aug. 20, 1792, m Apphia Kezer and Abigail Slack. Miriam, b Feb. 1, 1795, m Asa W. Soule. Elias, b June 24, 1800, m —— —— and Marinda Hale.

Thomas Whittier, m Waitstill Bishop, daughter of

Squier B. c Porter, b Oct. 17, 1781. Benjamin, b Aug. 21, 1783. Lois, b Dec. 2, 1785.

William Whittier, m Betsey Hankerson. c John, b May 25, 1775. Hannah, b Dec. 10, 1776. Sarah, b Aug. 13, 1778. Dorcas, b March 30, 1780. Polly Porter, b March 6, 1782. Betsey, b Jan. 6, 1784. Miriam, b Nov. 11. 1785.

Eliphalet Wight, m Abigail Besse. c Salome, b Sept. 10, 1795. Mary, b Jan. 20, 1797. Kezia, b Feb. 7, 1799.

Timothy Wight, m Sarah Fisher. c Sarah, b Jan 30, 1778. Jonathan, b Dec. 11, 1780. Benjamin, b Mar. 23, 1783. Joseph, b Mar. 9, 1787.

Ichabod Wing, m Elisabeth Prescot, daughter of Odlin P. c Lucy B. b July, 24, 1793, m Lewis Rowe. Leafy, b Sept. 15, 1795, m Cyrus Weston. Gorham Albion, b July, 15, 1798, M. D.

Andrew Wood, b in Middleborough, Mass. m Mary Camp. c John, b July 23, 1790, m Hannah Ward and Dolly Stevens. Armida, b Mar. 21, 1782, m Amasa Tinkham. Polly, b Feb. 26, 1794, m Jeremiah Smith. Christina, b Mar. 20, 1796, m Mordecai E. Morton. Andrew, Jr., b May 1, 1798, m Lydia Dole. Sumner, b Oct. 12, 1800, m Mary Andrews.

Elijah Wood, b in Middleborough, Mass., m Salley Clifford. c Samuel, b Dec. 1 1790, m Florena Sweet. Truxton, b Dec. 28, 1799, m Submit Blaisdell.

Enoch Wood, b in Middleboro', Mass., m Priscilla Camp. c Hannah, b Jan. 26, 1793, m James Pullen. Alonzo, b Feb. 6, 1795, m Abigail H. Branch. Selinda, b July 18, 1796, m David Eastman.

Henry Wood, jr., son of Moses, senior, m Eunice How, daughter of Ichabod H., Oct. 1, 1800.

Moses Wood, jr., m Nancy Esty. c Moses, 3d, b July 15, 1798.

Isaiah Wood, m Rebecca Perley, Jan. 6, 1799.

Jason Wood, m Desire ——. c Elizabeth, b Aug. 18, 1798.

Phinehas Wood, m Jedidah ——. c Theodata, b Sept. 4, 1794. Polly, b Dec. 1, 1797. Lucy, b April 27, 1800.

David Woodcock, m Mary Pullen, and Sarah Bragg. c of David and Mary. Liberty, b 1776. William, b September 13, 1780. Hannah, b September 16, 1782. Azi, b September 13, 1784. David, jr., b February 17, 1787. Polly, b May 30, 1789. James, b October 24, 1792, m Polly Monk. Josiah, b April 2, 1794, d July 27, 1816. Matthew, b November 22, 1796, m Sukey Monk, d June 10, 1836. Gustavus Adolphus, b April 10, 1799.

William Woodcock, m Lucy Buzzel, daughter of Jonathan B. c Melinda, b October 9, 1800.

James Work, m Esther Stevens. c Abel, b August 14, 1778. Polly, b April 28, 1780. Sally, b March 22, 1782, m John Lake. John, b July 13, 1785. Levi, b July 17, 1787. James, jr., b June 26, 1789. Lucy, b February 1, 1792. Joel, b July 1, 1794.

Abraham Wyman, m Dorothy ——. c Abraham, jr., b March 9, 1768. Thomas, b August 9, 1770. William, b April 11, 1774. Luther, b July 7, 1778. Luther, b September 9, 1780. Betsey, b February 25, 1785.

Daniel Wyman, m Ruth Wing. c John, b November 23, 1778. Daniel, jr., b September 5, 1780.

APPENDIX

TO THE

HISTORY OF WINTHROP.

APPENDIX.

NOTE A.

That posterity may know through what a long and formal process the early settlers had to pass, just to obtain a valid security to their lands, the following Deed is copied:—

To all to whom these Presents may come, Greeting.

Whereas his late Majesty King *James* the First, for the Advancement of a Colony and Plantation in *New-England*, in *America*, by his Highness's Letters Patents under the Great Seal of *England*, bearing Date at *Westminster*, the Third day of *November*, in the Eighteenth Year of his Highness's Reign of *England*, &c. did grant unto the Right Honourable *Lodowick*, late Lord Duke of *Lenox*, *George* late Lord Marquis of *Buckingham*, *James* Marquis of *Hamilton*, *Thomas* Earl of *Arundle*,

Robert Earl of *Warwick*, Sir *Ferdinando Georges*, Knt. and divers others whose names are expressed in the said Letters Patents, and their Successors, that they should be one Body Politick and Corporate, perpetually consisting of forty persons, that they should have perpetual Succession, and one Common Seal to serve for the said Body, and that they and their Successors should be incorporated, called and known by the Name of the Council established at *Plymouth*, in the County of *Devon*, for the planting, ruling, ordering and governing of *New-England*, in *America:* And further also did grant unto the said President and Council, and their Successors forever, under the Reservations in the said Letters Patents expressed; All that Part and Portion of the said Country called *New-England*, in *America*, situate, lying and being in Breadth from forty Degrees of Northerly Latitude from the Equinoctial Line, to forty-eight Degrees of the said Northerly Latitude inclusively, and in Length of and in all the Breadth aforesaid, throughout the Main Lands from Sea to Sea, together also, with all the firm Lands, Soils, Grounds, Creeks, Inlets, Havens, Ports, Seas, Rivers, Islands, Waters, Fishings, Mines, Minerals, precious Stones, Quarries, and all and singular the Commodities and Jurisdictions, both within the said Tract of Land lying upon the Main, as also within the said Islands and Seas adjoining: To have, hold, possess and enjoy the same unto the said Council and their Successors and Assigns forever, to be holden of his Majesty, his Heirs and Successors, as of his Manor, of *East-Greenwich*, in the County of *Kent*, in free and common Soccage, yielding and paying therefor to the said late King's Majesty, his Heirs and Successors, the fifth Part of the Ore of Gold and Silver as in and by the said Letters Patents, amongst other Privileges and Matters therein contained, more fully and at large it doth and may appear.

And Whereas the said Council established at *Plymouth* in the County of *Devon*, by their Charter and Deed of Affeofment bearing Date the Sixteenth Day of *January*, A. D. One Thousand Six Hundred and Twenty-Nine, by Virtue and Authority of his said late Majesty's Letters Patents, and for and in Consideration, that *William Bradford*, and his Associates had for these Nine Years lived in *New-England* aforesaid, and there inhabited and planted a Town called by the Name of *New-Plymouth*, at their own proper Cost and Charges; and seeing that by the special Providence of God, and their extraordinary Care and Industry, they had increased their Plantation to near three Hundred People, and were able to relieve any new Planters, or other His Majesty's Subjects upon that Coast; granted and assigned unto the said *William Bradford*, his Heirs, Associates and Assigns, all that Part of *New-England* in *America* aforesaid, and Tract and Tracts of Lands that lie within or between a certain Rivulet or Rundlet there, commonly called *Coahasset*, alias *Conahassett*, towards the North, and the River commonly called *Narragansett* River, towards the South, and the great Western Ocean towards the East, and between and within a straight Line directly extending up into the Main Land towards the West, from the Mouth of the said River, called *Narragansett River*, to the utmost Limits and Bounds of a Country or Place in *New-England* commonly called *Pocanacutt*, alias *Sawamset*, Westward, and another like straight Line extending itself directly from the Mouth of the said River called *Coahasset*, alias *Conahassett*, to the West, so far up into the Main Land Westward, as the utmost Limits of the said Place or Country commonly çalled *Pocanacutt*, alias *Sawamset*, do extend, together with one half of the said River called *Narragansett*, and the said Rivulet or Rundlet called *Coahasset*, alias *Conahassett*, and all Lands, Rivers, Waters, Havens, Creeks, Ports, Fishings, Fowlings, whatsoever, situate, lying and being, or arising within or between the said Limits and Bounds, or any of them.

And FOR AS MUCH as they had no convenient Place either of Trading or FISHING within their own Precincts, whereby after so long Travel and great Pains so hopeful a Plantation might subsist, as also that they might be encouraged the better to proceed in so pious a Work, which might especially tend to the Propagation of Religion, and the great Increase of Trade to his Majesty's Realms, and Advancement of the public Plantation;

The said Council further granted and assigned unto the said *William Bradford*, his Heirs, Associates and Assigns, ALL that Tract of Land, or Part of *New-England* in *America* aforesaid, which lieth within or between, and extendeth itself from the utmost limits of *Cobbiseconte*, alias *Comaseconte*, which adjoineth to the River of *Kennebeck*, alias *Kenebekike*, towards the Western Ocean, and a Place called the Falls, at *Neguamkike*, in *America* aforesaid, and the space of fifteen *English* miles on each side of the said River commonly called *Kennebeck* River, and all the said River called *Kennebeck*, that lies within the said Limits, and Bounds Eastward, Westward, Northward or Southward last above-mentioned, and all Lands' Grounds, Soils, Rivers, Waters, Fishings, situate, lying and being, arising, happening or accruing in or within the said Limits and Bounds, or either of them, together with all Rights and Jurisdictions thereof, the Admiralty Jurisdiction excepted, in as free, large, ample and beneficial Manner, to all Intents, Constructions and Purposes whatsoever, as the said Council by virtue of his Majesty's Letters Patents might or could grant.

TO HAVE AND TO HOLD the said Tract and Tracts of Lands, and all and singular the Premises above-mentioned to be granted, with their and every of their Appurtenances to the said *William Bradford*, his Heirs, Associates and Assigns forever, to the only proper and absolute Use and Behoof of the said *William Bradford*, his Heirs, Associates and Assigns forever, yielding and paying unto our said Sovereign Lord the King, his Heirs and Successors forever, one fifth Part of the Ore of the Mines of Gold and Silver, and one other fifth Part thereof to the President and Council which shall be had, possessed and obtained within the Precincts aforesaid, for all Services whatsoever, as in said Charter may more fully appear.

And whereas the said *William Bradford* and his Associates, afterwards assigned over and snrrendered up to the late Colony of *New-Plymouth*, the aforesaid Tract on

Kennebeck River, together with other Lands; and the same Colony afterwards, *viz.* on the Twenty-seventh Day of *October*, A. D. 1661, being seized of the whole Tract aforesaid on *Kennebeck* River, and also the Lands on both sides the said River, upwards to *Wisserunscut*, alias *Wesserunskick*, by their Deed of Bargain and Sale of that Date, for and in Consideration of the Sum of FOUR HUNDRED POUNDS *Sterling*, sold all the said Lands on said River to *Antipas Boyes*, *Edward Tyng*, *Thomas Brattle* and *John Winslow*, their and every of their Heirs and Assigns forever, as by the said Deed registered in the Records of said Colony may more fully appear. And the Lands last mentioned in said Deed by a Release and Confirmation were afterwards confirmed to the said *John Winslow* and his Partners aforesaid, their Heirs and Assigns forever, on both Sides of said *Kennebeck* River as far up as the upper or most Northern Part of *Wesserunskick* aforesaid. KNOW YE, THAT WE, the Heirs and Assigns of the said *Antipas Boyes*, *Edward Tyng*, *Thomas Brattle* and *John Winslow*, of and in all said Lands on *Kennebeck* River aforesaid, and legal Proprietors thereof, at our Meeting held at *Boston*, this Twelfth Day of *April*, A. D. 1769, called and regulated according to Law, have voted, granted and asssigned to *JOHN CHANDLER*, of a place called *Pond Town*, in the County of *Lincoln* and Province of *Massachusetts Bay*, in *New-England*, yeoman, his Heirs and Assigns forever, a lot of Land in said *Pond Town*, being one mile long and one hundred poles wide, and containing two hundred acres, and is lot Number forty-eight, as per plan of said Township will appear, but upon the following conditions viz. That the said *John Chandler* build an house not less than twenty feet square and seven feet stud, clear, and bring to, fit for tillage, five acres of land within three years from the date hereof, and actually live and dwell upon the premises himself during said term; or in case of his death, that his heirs, or some person under them shall dwell thereupon for seven years after the expiration of said three years; also work upon the Ministerial lot, or in building the House for the public Worship of God, two days in a year for ten years to come, when required by the Standing Committee of this Propriety, or their agent; also two days in a year upon the Public Lands until said Lands shall be incorporated into a Township, and also that he submit himself, relating to all Town affairs, to what shall be Voted by the major part of the settlers, (of said Pond Town,) at any meeting duly called. Reserving to this Propriety all mines and minerals whatsoever within the hereby granted premises, with liberty of digging and carrying off the same.

AND for the better perpetuating the aforesaid Vote and Grant of said Lands to the said *John Chandler*, his Heirs and Assigns for ever, We the said Proprietors at our said Meeting have further Voted, that the Clerk of this Propriety for the Time being be, and he hereby is directed and authorized, at the Request and Cost of the above-named Grantee, unto our said Votes and Grant of the Lands aforesaid, to affix the common Seal of said Propriety, and as Clerk as aforesaid, to acknowledge before any Justice in said Commonwealth the said Votes and Grant to be the Votes and Grant of said Proprietors for the purpose above-mentioned, and the Seal hereto affixed, to be the common Seal of said Propriety.

HENRY ALLINE, JUN'R, { *Clerk of said Propriety.*

SUFFOLK *ss.* *Boston,* The twelfth Day of May, A. D. 1769.

[L. S.] THIS Day personally appeared HENRY ALLINE, JUN'R, Clerk of the Proprietors of the *Kennebeck* Purchase from the late Colony of *New-Plymouth,* and acknowledged the above-mentioned Votes and Grant to be the Votes and Grant of said Proprietors to the within named *John Chandler.* And the Seal hereto by him affixed as Clerk as aforesaid, to be the Common Seal of said Propriety.

Before me, JOHN HILL, *Justice of the Peace.*

LINCOLN, *ss.* Received Septem'r 27th, 1774 and recorded with the Records for Deeds in said County, Lib. 2d, Fol. 236.

Att'st: JONA. BOWMAN, *Reg.*

All the first settlers had Deeds similar to this.

NOTE B.

Anno Regni Regis Georgio Tertio Undecimo.

ACT OF INCORPORATION.

Whereas, the Inhabitants of a certain Tract of land called Pond Town, lying on the west side of Kennebec River, in the County of Lincoln, are desirous of enjoying the Privileges that will arise to them by being incorporated into a town,

Be it enacted by the Governor, Council and House of Representatives, that the Tract of land aforesaid, butted and bounded as follows, viz: Beginning on the west side of Cobbesseconte great Pond, at the easterly end of the southerly line of a two hundred acre lot numbered one; from thence to run a west-north-west course five miles; from thence to run a north-north-east course about nine miles, until it meets a line running west-north-west from the north-west corner of the town of *Hallowell;* from thence to run east-north-east on the last mentioned line seven miles more or less, to the north-west corner of the said town; and from thence to run southerly on the west line of said town as far as the northerly end of Cobbesseconte great Pond; from thence to run westerly on the northerly end of said Pond to the west side thereof;

thence to run southerly on the westerly side of said Pond to the first mentioned boundary; containing also the said Pond as far south as the boundary, be and hereby is enacted into a township by the name of Winthrop; and that the Inhabitants thereof be and hereby are invested with all the Powers, Privileges and Immunities which the Inhabitants of any of the Towns within this Province do, or by law ought to enjoy.

And be it further enacted, that James Howard, Esq. be and hereby is empowered to issue his warrant directed to some principal Inhabitant in said Township, requiring him to notify and warn the Inhabitants in said Township, qualified by law to vote in Town affairs, to meet at such time and place as shall be therein set forth, to choose all such officers as shall be necessary to manage the affairs of said Township.

And be it further enacted, that the freeholders of the said Town shall be and hereby are empowered, at their first meeting, to proceed to bring in their votes for Register of Deeds, and also for a Treasurer for the said County of Lincoln, qualified according to law; and the votes for such Register and Treasurer shall be at the same time sealed up by a Constable of said Town, who may then be chosen and sworn, and by him returned into the Court of General Sessions of the Peace, to be holden in June next, at Pownalborough, for the said County, in the same manner as is provided by law in like cases for other Towns within this Province; which Court is hereby authorized and required to receive the said votes, which votes with the votes of the other Towns of said County, shall be opened, sorted and counted, as the law directs, for the determining the choice of such Register and Treasurer, and such choice shall be to all intents and purposes valid and effectual in law.

And be it further enacted, that if by reason of sickness, or any other means, the said James Howard, Esq. shall be prevented from performing the business, (or any part thereof,) to which he is appointed by this act, then, in that case, William Cushing, Esq. shall be and hereby is empowered to transact the whole, or any part of said business, as fully and effectually as the said James Howard is by the several clauses of this act, empowered to transact the same.

April 26, 1771.—This bill having been read three several times in the House of Representatives, passed to be enacted.

Thomas Cushing, *Speaker.*

April 26, 1771.—This bill having been read three several times in Council, passed to be enacted.

Thomas Flucker, *Sec'y.*

April 26, 1771.—By the Governor. I consent to the enacting of this bill.

T. Hutchinson.

Attest: Wm. Tudor, *Secretary of the State.*

The leaf of the Town Records containing a copy of the warrant for the first Town meeting, is torn, and part of it lost. The date and signature are as follows: —

"Given under my hand and seal, the sixth day of May, 1771, at Fort Western, James Howard, *Justice of Peace.*"

From the fragments of the Town Records, it is inferred, that this warrant was directed to Mr. John Chandler, who, in obedience to instructions, warned a meeting of the inhabitants to be held on the 20th of May.

NOTE C.

It may gratify the curiosity of some to know the ancient formalities of calling a Town meeting.

FEBRUARY, ye. 3d. A. D., 1772.

"The select men met and ordered the Town Clerk to issue his warrant to Stephen Pullen, Constable, to warn the Freeholders and other Inhabitants of the Town of Winthrop duly qualified by Law to vote in Town affairs, to meet at the house of Squier Bishop, Innholder, in said Town on Monday the second day of March next, at nine o'clock in the morning, then and there, if the Town see cause, to act upon the following particulars, viz :

Then follows an enumeration of six particulars. The town Clerk's warrant was as follows :

LINCOLN, ss. *To Stephen Pullen, Constable of the town of Winthrop, within the County of Lincoln, Greeting :*

In his Majesty's name you are required to warn the Freeholders and other Inhabitants of the Town of Winthrop duly qualified by Law to vote in town affairs to meet at the house of Squier Bishop, Innholder, in said Town on Monday the second day of march next at nine o'clock in the morning, then and there, if the Town see cause to act upon the following articles.

I. To choose Town Officers to serve the town the year ensuing.

II. To hear the Report of the Selectmen respecting the highways they have laid out the year past and to confirm the same if they shall see cause.

III. To pay the Town's just Debts.

IV. To order such names into the Box asthe Town shall think proper, to serve as Petit Jurors at the inferior court of Common Pleas.

V. To choose a Committee to solicit Mr. Gardiner to open a place through or round his mill-dam to let the fish up for the benefit of the Town.

VI. To see if it be the minds of the Town to make and repair their highways by a Tax, and if so to raise money for the same.

Hereof fail not and make a return of this warrant with your doings hereon at one hour before the time set for the meeting.

By order of the Selectmen,

JONATHAN WHITING, *Town Clerk.*

Winthrop, Feb. ye. 3d, 1772."

NOTE D.

Names of the original members of the Congregational Church, organized Sept. 4, 1776.

Jonathan Whiting,	Nathaniel Stanley,
Elias Taylor,	Josiah Hall,
Joseph Stephens,	Ransford Smith.
Nathaniel Floyd,	Mary Taylor,
Samuel Frost,	Elizabeth Stevens,
John Chandler,	Sarah Floyd,
Pease Clark,	Abigail Stanley,
Thomas Allen,	Sarah Delano,
Jonathan Davenport,	Abigail Hall,
Amos Stevens,	Dorcas Baker,
Ebenezer Davenport,	Mary Stevens,
Gideon Lambert,	Anne Hall,
Joseph Baker,	Susanna Lambert.

COVENANT adopted by the Congregational Church, at their organization, Sept. 4, 1776.

"We, being distant from any neighboring church, and desirous of having the ordinances of the gospel occasionally administered among us, till settled, which we hope will be soon, do enter into a church estate; and in the fear of God and under a humiliating sense of our own unworthiness to transact with the glorious God; and with a humble dependence on the grace of God, covenant with Him and with one another as followeth, viz:

First of all, we do solemnly avouch the Lord Jehovah,

Father, Son, and Holy Ghost, for our portion and chief good; and give up ourselves, bodies and souls, to Him, to be his servants, promising by his aid and assistance to love, fear and trust in Him, and yield obedience to Him in all things, all the days of our lives.

And whereas the Son of God, in our nature, is exalted as a Prince and Saviour, the only Mediator of the new covenant and means of coming to God, we do therefore, through grace *accept* of Him according to the tenor of the gospel offer, that is to say, of Prophet, Priest and King of our immortal souls, purposing and promising to attend his teaching, his word and Spirit, to lean upon his merits and intercession with the Father, as the only way for the obtainment of the pardon of our sins, the favor of God and continuance therein, and finally the subduing of all our enemies, and working all our works in us and for us.

And further, whereas there are different apprehensions in the minds of the great and wise men, even in the doctrines of religion, we do declare our consent to them, as held forth in the Westminster Confession of Faith, or Shorter Catechism, apprehending in our judgments and consciences, that they are agreeable to the holy Scriptures.

Again, whereas God has promised to be a God unto his people and their children after them, we do therefore dedicate our children to the service of God in Jesus Christ, promising that we will seasonably bring those of them, that are unbaptized, to Jesus Christ in the ordinance of baptism; and as they grow up in years of understanding, instruct them into the nature, use and end of that ordinance, and in the principles of the christian religion so far as need is, that we will set good examples of piety, righteousness and sobriety before them, restraining them, as we are able, from being carried away with the temptations of their age and time, endeavoring that they may be prepared for the enjoyment of Christ in all his ordinances; and finally be much in prayer for their conversion and salvation; and we further engage to watch over all the children of the covenant growing up with us, that they be obedient to the rule and government of our Lord Jesus Christ.

We promise that we will, by the help of God, avoid all the superstitions and inventions of men in the worship of God, as derogating from the sovereignty and wisdom of the Lord Jesus Christ, the supreme Head of the Church; that we will not slanderously absent ourselves from any part of the instituted worship, but do what in us lies to prepare ourselves for, to uphold and improve all the ordinances of Christ, to the spiritual benefit and advantage of our souls, leaning upon that promise, that God will meet those that rejoice, work righteousness and remember Him in his ways.

We promise, by the help of God, that we will, with as much frequency as may be, read or cause the word of God to be read in our families, that so the word of God may dwell richly in us, seasonably and constantly upholding the worship of God there and attending the same with sincerity and affection.

And whereas we have given ourselves unto the Lord and unto one another in the Lord, we propose and promise that we will live together in this holy fellowship, in all holy watchfulness over each other to the prevention of, or recovery from any scandalous evils, that through the temptations of satan or the corruptions of our own nature, we may at any time be overtaken with, that we will be as speedy as may be in making up any difference that may arise, in some orderly way, endeavoring also the spiritual and temporal good one of another.

We promise, that by the help of God, we will have respect to all the duties of the second table, as being necessary parts of a right ordered conversation, and particularly, be true and faithful to all our civil contracts and agreements with one another and all men that we have to deal with, so that none may have occasion to speak evil of our profession.

And finally, whereas there is a strong propensity in our nature to what is evil and sinful, we purpose and promise that, by the help of God's Spirit, we will keep our hearts and mortify those lusts that dwell in us, avoiding all such temptations as our sinful hearts are wont to be drawn aside withal; and that we may keep this covenant inviolable for ever in all the branches of it, we desire to deny ourselves, not trusting in our own wisdom or strength, humbly and believingly depending upon God in and through Jesus Christ, and the presence of his Holy Spirit with us, and where we come short, there to wait upon Him for pardon and healing for his namesake.

NOTE E.

Oct. 17, 1781, the town voted as encouragement to Rev. David Jewett to settle with us to give him the grant of a two hundred and sixty acre lot, and *sixty pounds* lawful money the first year, and the said salary to increase yearly as our interest increases, until it arrive to *eighty pounds*, the same to be estimated at Rye at 5s per bushel, Indian corn at 4s, and beef at 3d per pound, what money he shall receive towards his salary shall be in proportion to the aforesaid articles as herein stated. And to prevent all misunderstanding of this vote, it is the true intent and meaning of the same, that if said articles shall fall, the salary shall fall in proportion, but that his salary shall be paid in proportion to the above, said articles not exceeding the within price. The town voted to raise and pay Mr. Jewett £12 lawful money, probably for his services prior to his settlement.

Rev. David Jewett's answer to the call of the church and people of Winthrop to become their Pastor.

"And now Gentlemen of the town of Winthrop respecting your grant for the support of a public Teacher, you have done honorably and well; and have even exceeded my most sanguine desire. I therefore most cheerfully donate and refund one-twentieth of my annual salary during my ministry among you, for the support of a school, and to be distributed at the discretion of the Selectmen of the town; only shall expect to be absent two Sabbaths in a year for the purpose of visiting my friends at a distance; should I occasionally be absent longer than that term shall expect to refund it out of my yearly salary, sickness only excepted. Wishing you the blessing of God, the grace of our Lord Jesus Christ and the consolations of the Holy Spirit, I am your affectionate Friend and most humble servant.

DAVID JEWETT.

Dated at Winthrop, Nov. 16, 1781.

Whether a school was supported by this donation of Mr. Jewett is not known.

NOTE F.

An act to incorporate the north part of the Town of Winthrop, in the County of Lincoln, with the inhabitants thereon, into a Town by the name of Readfield.

SEC. 1. Be it enacted by the Senate and House of Representatives, in General Court assembled, and by the authority of the same, That all the lands in the town of Winthrop, lying north of the line hereafter described, viz: Beginning on the south line of lot number thirty-two in said Winthrop, where the west line of Hallowell crosses said lot, from thence running west-north-west, on the range line to Chandler's pond; then westerly across said pond to the south-east corner of lot number two hundred and twenty; then westerly on the south line of said lot; to south-west corner of said lot; then northerly to the north-east corner of lot number sixty-six; from thence west-north-west on the north line of lots number sixty-six, ninety-three, and one hundred fifty-six, to the westerly line of said town, with all the inhabitants thereon living, be, and hereby are incorporated into a separate town, by the name of Readfield, with all the powers, privileges and immunities, that towns within this Commonwealth have, or do enjoy.

SEC. 2. And be it further enacted by the authority aforesaid, That the inhabitants of the said town of Readfield shall be subject to, and pay all rates and taxes heretofore assessed upon them, while they belonged to the town of Winthrop, in the same manner as though this act had not been passed; and shall also be subject to pay their proportionable part of all debts due from said town of Winthrop, at the time of their separation, and also shall receive their proportionable part of all public lands, and of all other public property whatever, that did belong to said town of Winthrop, at the time of their separation.

Sec. 3. And be it further enacted that the said town of Readfield shall take and support their proportionable part of all the poor, that did belong to said town of Winthrop, at the time of their separation, according to their last valuation; and provided any person or persons have removed from said town of Winthrop, and shall be hereafter returned as the poor of said town; then and in such case the said town of Readfield shall take and support as their poor all those who immediately before such removal were the inhabitants of that part of the town of Winthrop, which is now Readfield.

Sec. 4. And be it further enacted by the authority aforesaid, that until the said town of Readfield shall have a sufficient number of inhabitants to entitle them to send a Representative, they shall assemble and meet with the town of Winthrop, and in town meeting alternately at Winthrop and Readfield shall join in choosing a Representative to serve in the General Court of this Commonwealth.

Sec. 5. And be it enacted by the authority aforesaid,

that Jonathan Whiting, Esq., be, and he hereby is authorized and empowered to issue his warrant to some principal inhabitant of the said town of Readfield requiring him to notify and warn said inhabitants to meet at some convenient time and place in said Readfield, to choose all such officers as other towns by law are required to choose in the month of March or April annually.

This act passed March 11, 1791.

NOTE G.

An Act to incorporate a number of the inhabitants of the town of Winthrop into a religious society by the name of the First Congregational Society in Winthrop.

Sect. 1. *Be it enacted* by the Senate and House of Representatives in General Court assembled, and by the authority of the same, that—

Samuel Wood,
Joseph Metcalf,
Nathaniel Fairbanks,
Nathaniel Smith,
Moses Frost,
Nathaniel Morton,
John Chandler, Jr.,
Micah Barrows,
Reuben Brainard,
Noah Morrill,
Isaac Smith,
Jonathan Whiting,
Jonathan Whiting, Jun.,
James Prescott,
Solomon Esty,
John White,
John Kezer,
Henry Wood,
Elijah Davenport,
Amos Perley,
Samuel Morrell,
Jonathan Currier,
John Turner,
James Atkinson,
Solomon Towle,
David Chandler,
John Streeter,
Jonathan Thurston,
Richard Gower,
Zebediah Sweet,
Peleg Benson,
Henry Stanley,
Josiah Bacon,
Moses Joy,
Peter Stanley,
Solomon Stanley,

Enoch Wood,
Joseph Matthews,
Barzillai Delano,
Adin Stanley,
Simon Page,
Simon Page, Jun.,
Odlin Prescott,
Elijah Wood,
Sampson Davis,
Jonathan Pullen,
Peter Gale,
John Cole,
Josiah Cushman,
Benjamin Read,
Livy Morton,
Ebenezer Morton,
Charles Harris,
Ebenezer Moore,
Jenness Towle,
Amos Stevens,
Amos Stevens, Jun.,
Daniel Stevens,
Unite Brown,
William Brown,
Jonas Stevens,
William Stevens,
Ebenezer Davenport,
Thomas Ladd,
Nathaniel Fellows,
Jeremiah Brown,
Andrew Wood,
Nathaniel Marston,
Jonathan Hilliard,
John May,
Silas Lambert,
William Pullen,
Mordecai Morton,
Gideon Lambert,
Moses Wood,
Jesse Sweet,
Nathan Richmond,
Daniel Marrow, Jun.,
Jonathan Pullen, Jun.,
Josiah Tilton,
Isaac Shaw,
James Pullen,
Elijah Prescott,
Ebenezer Barrows,
John Pullen,
Liberty Stanley,
Obed Leach,
Abiel Smith,
Squier Bishop, and
Stephen Pullen,

together with their polls and estates, be and they are hereby incorporated into a Society by the name of the First Congregational Society in Winthrop, with all the privileges, powers and immunities, to which Parishes are, by law, entitled in this Commonwealth.

Sect. 2—described the way of becoming members.

Sect. 3—authorized Samuel Wood, Esq. to issue his warrant to call the first meeting, &c.

Passed January 31, 1800.

NOTE H.

REV. JONATHAN BELDEN.

The Ecclesiastical Council who ordained Mr. Belden, were Rev. Messrs. Ezekiel Emerson, Georgetown; Samuel Eaton, Harpswell; Eliphalet Gillet, Hallowell; Jonathan Ward, New Milford, (now Alna;) Jotham Sewall, Chesterville. Delegates, Benjamin Dunning, Mark Langdon Hill, Henry Sewall, Jonathan B. Balch, James Rowe, Isaiah Wyman, Dummer Sewall, James Gow. Rev. J. Sewall led in the first prayer, Rev. E. Gillet preached, Rev. E. Emerson led in the ordaining prayer, Rev. S. Eaton gave the charge, Rev. J. Ward gave the right hand, Rev. S. Eaton led in the closing prayer. More than forty had been members of the church, but probably at this time, the number was less than twenty. Some forty-three were added during Mr. Belden's ministry, of five years. He was, after this, pastor of the church in Bristol for several years.

After leaving Bristol, he was not pastor of any church. He was employed in several places, as a Missionary, and died some years ago. He was "a man who feared God above many."

REV. DAVID THURSTON.

The members of the Council who ordained David Thurston to the pastoral office, were, from the church in

Hallowell, Eliphalet Gillet, pastor, Henry Sewall and James Gow, Delegates; from the church in Byfield, Mass., Elijah Parish, pastor, Joseph Pike and Solomon Stickney, Delegates; from the church in New Castle, Kiah Bayley, pastor; from the church in Penobscot, Jonathan Powers, pastor; from the 1st church in Bath, Asa Lyman, pastor, David Trufant and Henry Sewall, jr., Delegates; from the church in Bucktown, (now Bucksport,) Mighill Blood, pastor; from the church in Sedgwick, David Thurston, sen., Delegate; from the church in New Milford, Joseph Richardson, Delegate. Rev. A. Lyman offered the introductory prayer, Rev. E. Parish preached from 2 Cor. 2 : 15, Rev. J. Powers offered the consecrating prayer, Rev. E. Gillet gave the charge, Rev. M. Blood gave the right hand, and Rev. K. Bayley offered the concluding prayer.

REV. R. M. SAWYER.

The Ecclesiastical Council at the ordination of Rev. Rufus Morrell Sawyer, were, from the church in Augusta South, Bro. G. H. Jones; Bridgton Center, Rev. J. T. Hawes; Gardiner, Rev. W. L. Hyde; Hallowell, Rev. J. P. Skeele, Bro. Paul Stickney; Litchfield, Rev. T. Davis, Dea. Isaac Smith; Otisfield, Rev. J. P. Richardson, Bro. L. M. Sawyer; Richmond, Rev. P. F. Barnard, Bro. G. C. Waterman; Searsport, Rev. S. Thurston, Dea. Benjamin Gould; Waterville, Rev. R. B. Thurston, Bro. S. R. Dennen. Also, Rev. B. Tappan, D. D., and Rev. Prof. Shepard. The parts at this ordination, were performed as follows: Invocation by Rev. J. T. Hawes, reading the Scriptures by Rev. R. B. Thurston, introductory prayer by Rev. P. F. Barnard, sermon by Prof. Shepard from Acts 14 : 1, consecrating prayer by Rev. J. P. Richardson, charge to the pastor by the former pastor, right hand of fellowship by Rev. J. P. Skeele, the concluding prayer by Rev. S. Thurston.

NOTE I.

"An act to incorporate a number of the inhabitants of the town of Winthrop into a religious society by the name of the Methodist Society in the town of Winthrop.

SECTION 1.—*Be it enacted by the Senate and House of Representatives in General Court assembled, and by the authority of the same,* that

Nathaniel Bishop,	Alfred Chandler,
Thomas Jacobs,	Daniel Marrow,
Benjamin Fairbanks,	Timothy Foster,
Rial Stanley,	Enos Fairbanks,
Asa Robbins,	David Fairbanks,
Eleazar Robbins,	Benjamin Fairbanks, jr.,
Otis Foster,	Jonas Allen,
Daniel Foster,	Elizabeth Lake,
Nathan F. Cobb,	

together with such others as have already associated, or may hereafter associate with them and their successors, be, and hereby are incorporated into a separate religious society by the name of the Methodist Society in Winthrop, with all the powers and privileges and subject to the same duties with other religious societies, according to the Constitution and laws of this Commonwealth.

Provided, however, that all such persons shall be holden to pay their respective proportions of all moneys legally assessed for parochial purposes in the Parish or religious society, to which he or she formerly belonged.

SEC. 2. — *Be it enacted &c.*, that any person belonging to another religious society in said town of Winthrop, who may desire to join with the said Methodist Society, shall declare such intention in writing, delivered to the minister or clerk thereof, and also a copy of the same delivered to the town clerk, or to the clerk of such other society (as the case may require,) and if such person do produce such a certificate signed by the minister, deacon, or clerk of the said Methodist Society, that he or she has united with, and actually become a member thereof, such person shall, from the date of said certificate, be considered, with his or her polls and estates, as a member of said Methodist Society.

SEC. 3. — *Be it enacted &c.*, that when any member of said Methodist Society shall see cause to secede therefrom and to unite in religious fellowship with any other religious society, shall give notice of such intention in writing to the minister or clerk of the said Methodist Society, and deliver a copy of the same to the clerk of the town or to the minister or clerk of such other society, (as the case may be,) fifteen days before the annual meeting, and shall produce a certificate of admission, signed by the minister or clerk thereof, such person with his or her polls and estate shall, from the date of such certificate, be considered as a member of the society, with which he or she has so united."

Section 4 contains directions for calling a meeting and organizing the Society.

"This act passed, Feb. 27, 1811.

Methodist Preachers who have officiated since the building of their Chapel.

1826, Rev. Stephen Lovell.	1841, D. B. Randall.
1827, "	1842, E. Robinson.
1828, J. B. Husted.	1843, "
1829, Moses Hill	1844, A. F. Barnard.
1830, "	1845, "
1831, E. Crooker.	1846, George Webber.
1832, G. Greely.	1847, Charles W. Morse.
1833, D. Fuller.	1848, "
1834, A. Caldwell.	1849, Moses Hill.
1835, "	1850, "
1836, C. P. Bragdon.	1851, Parker Jaquis.
1837, E. Hotchkiss.	1852, "
1838, A. P. Hillman.	1853, C. Munger.
1839, Abel Alton.	1854, "
1840, J. Cleaveland.	1855, J. H. Jennie.

NOTE K.

Names of persons who were organized into the first Baptist Church in Winthrop.

Enoch Wood,	Ebenezer Blake,
Benjamin Packard,	Isaac Wadsworth,
Joseph Wingate, Jr.,	David Eastman,
Ebenezer Packard,	Nancy Smith,
Francis Fuller,	Elizabeth Swift,
Luke Perkins,	Nancy Packard,
Benjamin Perkins,	Zeruiah Packard,
Joshua Smith,	Hannah Easty,
William Jamerson,	Sarah T. White,
John Wadsworth, Jr.,	Sarah B. Pullen,
Joseph Wood,	Zeruiah Matthews,
William Hughs,	Joanna Richards,
Joseph Packard.	Clarissa Richards,
Liberty Woodcock,	Amelia Whiting,
Samuel Shaw,	Lucretia Richards.

Males, 18; Females, 12; Total, 30.

The same day "Brothers Joshua Smith, Enoch Wood, and Luke Perkins were chosen Deacons, and ordained by prayer and imposition of hands."

REV. J. H. INGRAHAM.

At the ordination of Rev. J. H. Ingraham, Feb. 23d, 1836, the services were as follows: "Invocation by Bro.

Case. Reading the Scriptures by Bro. Robinson. Sermon by President Babcock. Consecrating prayer by Bro. Low. Charge to the Pastor by Bro. Drinkwater. Right hand of fellowship by Bro. S. F. Smith. Concluding prayer by Bro. Barrows. Benediction by the Pastor,

REV. F. MERRIAM.

The exercises at the ordination of Rev. F. Merriam were as follows: Invocation and reading the Scriptures by Bro. O. B. Walker. Introductory prayer by David Thurston. Sermon by Rev. Mr. Nott. Ordaining prayer by Rev. Mr. Grant. Charge by Rev. S. F. Smith. Right hand of fellowship by Rev. Mr. Williams. Charge to the church and people by Rev. Mr. Adlam. Concluding prayer by Rev. Mr. Piper. Benediction by the Pastor.

REV. MR. POWERS.

The exercises at the ordination of Mr. Powers were as follows; Reading of Scriptures by Rev. Mr. Merriam. Introductory prayer by Father Case. Sermon by Rev. D. N. Sheldon, D. D. Ordaining prayer by Rev. A. Drinkwater. Right hand of fellowship by Rev. S. W. Field. Charge to Pastor by Rev. A. Kallock. Address to the church by Rev. William Tilley. Concluding prayer by David Thurston. Benediction by the Pastor.

NOTE L.

Names of the members of the Universalist church.

Rev. Giles Baily and wife,
Rev. Comfort C. Smith and wife,
Nathan Howard and wife,
James Bowdoin Fillebrown and wife,
Mrs. Nancy Richmond,
Shepherd Bean,
Mrs. Oliver Bean,
Noah Currier,
John Elliot Snell and wife,
Benjamin Perkins Briggs and wife,
Mrs. Lewis Wood,
Mrs. Lewis Cobb,
Mrs. Sophronia Chandler,
Lucy Chandler,
Azel Perkins and wife,
Francis Perley,
Nathan Fisher Cobb and wife,
Benjamin Robbins and wife,

Jerusha Robbins,
Rev. Benjamin Franklin Robbins and wife,
Hiram Pitts,
George G. Fairbanks,
Mrs. Polly Stanley.

Of late they have not had the ordinance of the Lord's supper administered to them.

NOTE M.

CONSTITUTION.

ARTICLE. 1. This society shall be styled the Winthrop Society for the Promotion of Good Morals.

ART. 2. The objeet of this society shall be to promote good morals and discountenance vice universally, particularly to discourage profaneness, idleness, gross breaches of the Sabbath, and intemperance.

ART. 3. If any member of this society shall be guilty of those immoralities, which it is the intention of this society to reform, he shall be reproved by the society, and puon a second conviction of similar conduct, his name shall be erased from the constitution, as unworthy a standing in the society.

ART. 4. Any person who shall subscribe this constitution and pay *annually* for the purchase of suitable tracts for the accomplishment of the above object, shall be a member of the society.

ART. 5. The stated meetings of the society shall be on the last Mondays of March and September annually, at the Meeting-house, at two o'clock P. M. Seven members shall constitute a quorum, with power of adjournment to any time not specified above.

ART. 6, At the meeting on the last Monday in March

or September, there shall be elected, in such manner as may be agreed, a President whose duty it shall be to preside in all meetings of the society, a Corresponding Secretary, a Recording Secretary, a Treasurer, and a Committee of five persons to receive and communicate information, to arrange the business of the society at their several meetings, and to report from time to time the result of such measures as shall have been taken.

Art. 7. The Committee, when notified by their chairman, shall meet at such time and place as he may appoint, to consult on the general objects of the society, and to carry into execution any of its regulations.

Art. 8. Each member shall consider himself bound to endeavor by counsel, persuasion and warning, and by other kind and prudent methods, to reclaim the vicious. He shall likewise prudently endeavor, by his own example and advice, to discourage the improper use of ardent spirits within the sphere of his influence, and duly to restrain his children and those under his care on the Lord's day.

Art. 9. This Constitution may be altered at either of the stated meetings by the concurrence of two-thirds of the members present.

Art. 10. Every meeting of this society shall be opened and closed by prayer.

The Society were conscious of their insufficiency to effect the reformation they desired. Their dependence was on God. They therefore sought Him, at the opening of their meetings, that he would guide them to adopt the right means; and, at their close, that he would give success to the means they employed.

POSTING TIPPLERS &c.

An act for the regulation of licensed houses, passed Feb. 28, 1789.

SECTION 16. Be it further enacted by the authority aforesaid, that the Selectmen in each town shall cause to be posted up in the houses and shops of all taverners, innholders, and retailers, as aforesaid, in such towns or districts, a list of the names of all persons reputed common drunkards, or common tipplers, or common gamesters, misspending their time and estate in such houses. Every keeper of such house or shop, after notice given him as aforesaid, that shall be convicted before one or more Justices of the peace, of entertaining or suffering any of the persons in such list, to drink, or tipple, or game in his or her house, or any of the dependencies thereof, or of selling them spirituous liquors as aforesaid shall forfeit and pay the sum of thirty shillings.

NOTE N.

A copy of the Constitution of the Society for Mutual Improvement.

ART. 1. This society shall be called THE SOCIETY FOR MUTUAL IMPROVEMENT.

ART. 2. Every member of this society pledges herself to consider the import of those commands given to christians to come out from the world and be separate, and spend a part of every Saturday evening as a season of meditation upon the various duties that belong to the wife of a minister, and also to ask the blessing of God upon the efforts of this society.

ART. 3. As women professing godliness, the members of this Society engage to guard against the "Lust of the eye and the pride of life," and to retrench in articles of dress, furniture, and table luxuries, so as to come nearer to the requisitions of the gospel, and to use their influence in accordance with these principles.

ART. 4. It shall likewise be the duty of every member of this Society to make efforts for the establishment of Maternal Associations, and to connect with these associations endeavors for the best good of domestics and dependents as well as children — to encourage female prayer meetings, to interest herself in Sabbath School instruction, and in all the various benevolent societies that call for the aid of the churches, and make an annual report of her labors to the secretary.

ART, 5. The officers of this society shall be a first and second Directress, a Secretary and Treasurer. The lady who holds the two last-mentioned offices, with the first and second Directress, shall constitute a Board of Managers.

ART. 6. Any clergyman's wife may become a member of this Society by subscribing to these articles.

www.ingramcontent.com/pod-product-compliance
Lightning Source LLC
LaVergne TN
LVHW020056110826
845151LV00005B/1494